PLEASANT HILL

HYDROPONICS
soilless gardening explained

D0752258

Hydroponics

soilless gardening explained

Les Bridgewood

CONTRA COSTA COUNTY LIBRARY

3 1901 04233 3635

The Crowood Press

First published in 2003 by
The Crowood Press Ltd
Ramsbury, Marlborough
Wiltshire SN8 2HR

www.crowood.com

This impression 2005

© Les Bridgewood 2003

All rights reserved. No part of this publication may be reproduced or
transmitted in any form or by any means, electronic or mechanical, including
photocopy, recording, or any information storage and retrieval system, without
permission in writing from the publishers.

British Library Cataloguing-in-Publication Data

A catalogue record for this book is available from the British Library.

ISBN 1 86126 560 3

Line drawings by Keith Field.

Dedication
To my wife, Anne.

Typeset by Servis Filmsetting Ltd, Manchester

Printed and bound in Singapore by Craft Print International

Contents

Preface

Hydroponics can be defined as the science of growing plants in an environment other than soil and supplying them with essential nutrients dissolved in water. The aim of hydroponics is to provide the perfect environment around a plant's roots. This book will therefore be of interest to the gardener who wishes to move away from the problems created by growing plants in an imperfect soil-based environment. Natural fertilizer in soil depends on what the animal has been eating, how long the fertilizer has been left for bacteria and soil pests to break it down, and the conditions in which it has been stored. To feed a plant growing in soil a perfect balance of nutrients without including pests from natural fertilizer is virtually impossible. While most plants will manage under such conditions, how much better would they grow if presented with a balanced feed of nutrients in a pest-free environment?

Hydroponics has other practical advantages. Gardeners with back or other problems affecting their mobility will benefit from the flexibility of the system designs available. For example, growing plants in house guttering on a table at the correct height saves bending down, and a wheelchair could easily be used alongside a table adjusted to the required height.

In the field of education the uses of hydroponics are numerous, in particular for teaching children about the life cycle of plants.

While it is possible to grow plants hydroponically in the home, by installing the correct system in a greenhouse or utilizing an otherwise unusable area of concrete, the available growing area can be increased considerably. Information and ideas for an automated greenhouse are included in this book, along with tips such as how to grow tomatoes over winter.

CHAPTER 1

Introduction to Hydroponics

Since the beginning of civilization, soil has been considered the basic requirement for the cultivation of plants. However, soil comes in many grades, from being rich in nutrients to impoverished, and when combined with the problems presented by pests, life becomes somewhat of a lottery for plants. Growers over the ages have added substances to soil in attempts to improve the quality and quantity of harvests. The function of soil to a plant is more than just a means of enabling it to stand upright. It must make available every major and trace element required by the plant's roots, along with warm, oxygenated water. Air around the roots is also vital to successful plant growth, a fact that is often ignored. Plant roots also give off unwanted gases, which must be removed. The vegetation of the plant has demands as well, such as the correct climate along with air containing carbon dioxide around its leaves. Although the introduction of greenhouses has greatly improved a plant's chances of existing in a beneficial environment, in the near ideal world of hydroponics, optimum conditions are available to a plant and its roots all the time.

HISTORY OF HYDROPONICS

People have been unwittingly practising hydroponics for centuries, but the first recorded experiments to find out exactly what nutrients plants require to grow are attributed to John Woodward in 1699. However, it was not until the nineteenth century, with the intervening advances in scientific knowledge and equipment, that real progress was made.

A hydroponic harvest.

Wall unit, no nightly watering.

The well-documented experiments of the German plant scientists, Sachs (1860) and Knop (1861–65), in which they made synthetic solutions of the essential plant nutrients, formed the basis of present-day hydroponics. Research continued, especially in the United States in the early twentieth century, resulting in the publication of nutrient formulae and methods of growing. Commercial hydroponics essentially began in California in the 1930s, with the work of Dr W.F. Gericke. He set up large tanks filled with nutrient solutions, in which he grew tomatoes. Combined with the warm, sunny Californian climate, his tomatoes were a spectacular success. In 1945, the US Air Force provided fresh vegetables grown in a number of hydroponic sites for its personnel on Ascension Island in the South Atlantic. The island was barren and all fresh produce would have had to be transported. This also occurred on Wake Island in the Pacific Ocean, where small growing beds were constructed to provide fresh produce. The US Army used crushed volcanic rock as the medium in a hydroponic system on Iwo Jima. In 1945, the Air Ministry in the UK also constructed hydroponic growing units in Bahrain in the Persian Gulf and in Iraq at Habbaniya. Since the success of hydroponics in providing food for troops during World War II, research into hydroponics has been carried out at numerous institutions, including the University of Reading, Imperial Chemical Industries Ltd and the Glasshouse Research Institute in Sussex, England, eventually leading to the considerable success and popularity, both commercial and amateur, of hydroponics in its various forms.

THE BASICS OF HYDROPONICS

Hydroponics enables the grower to produce huge crops of cucumbers, peas, tomatoes, melons, potatoes, peppers and pineapples and other produce without a great deal of effort. Fantastic displays of flowers can be produced without the nightly need for watering. All these can be cultivated on a veranda, a flat roof or even in a spare room – no need for a garden.

Different plants have different requirements, and should be treated as individuals. Some like a low pH (acid-loving plants), others dislike cooler environments, some dislike strong light and so on. It is up to the grower to apply any knowledge possessed about the requirements of the foliage (air environment) of a particular type of plant. Hydroponics pays particular attention to the environment around the roots – the acidity (pH), the solution strength (the conductive Factor, or cF) and the solution temperature can all be finely controlled. The solution strength is measured by passing a very small electric current through the nutrient solution being fed to the plants; this is given a value referred to as the conductive Factor of that particular solution. As the plants take out nutrients the solution moves towards being an insulator (the cF falls) and less current flows in the solution. (For further information on cF and pH and a useful list of cF values for different plants, *see* Chapter 3.)

GROWING CONDITIONS REQUIRED BY PLANT LIFE

All plants have basic growing requirements, which should be adjusted according to the needs of the individual plant.

1. A warm air temperature.
2. The required duration of light (natural or artificial) at a good intensity along with, and just as important, the required periods of darkness.
3. Good levels of carbon dioxide in the air, but only *during periods of light*. This can be up to four times the amount found in fresh air.
4. A plentiful supply of oxygen in the solution around the roots along with a good airflow to remove gases generated by the roots.
5. The correct strength of solution (cF) around the roots for the type of plant being grown with a good balance of nutrients.
6. A warm solution around the roots to match the type of plant.
7. The pH (potential Hydrogen) of the solution should be in the correct range for the type of plant being grown.
8. High air humidity affects the rate of uptake of water or water and nutrients in the plant. During transpiration, the plant passes water vapour into the air. If the humidity is high the air may have as much moisture as it can hold and the ability to pass this water vapour may be interrupted. The commercial grower deals with the problem of humidity by employing vapour pressure deficit, which involves increasing the air temperature. The warmer the air the more moisture it can hold. The air temperature is increased until the temperature is high enough to make the vents in the greenhouse open, thereby facilitating a change of air.

DIFFERENT HYDROPONIC MEDIA

When a plant is grown hydroponically, the soil around it is replaced with an inert medium that contains no nutrients of its own, such as baked clay balls, coarse river sand, coarse sawdust, coir, foam, gravel, Hortifibre, perlite, pumice, Rockwool, straw or vermiculite. All of these media give the grower control over the pH, along with the nutrients they contain, while also giving a good ratio between the solution and air. However, a few of these substances, such as Hortifibre, sawdust and straw, are only good for short-term use as they decompose over time, thereby reducing the solution-to-air ratio.

---

pH (POTENTIAL HYDROGEN)

The pH (potential Hydrogen) is used to describe very small concentrations of hydrogen ions. The greater the number of H^+ ions in the solution, the more acid the solution will test and vice versa. Potential Hydrogen (pH) is usually given as from 1 to 14, with pH7 as neutral. A pH of 14 would be very alkaline, while a pH of 1 would be very acid (lots of H^+ ions).

Depending on the intended crop (root vegetables or leafy plants), mixes of the above media will be used to suit the plant being grown. Other media, such as crushed brick and coarse volcanic dust can be used, depending upon availability. Any mixture must be well-draining and completely inert, and the pH must be under the control of the grower. If bricks or any medium used have been in contact with lime or may contain this substance, then they are not suitable for hydroponics. Plants can even be grown without using any sort of medium, using a method known as the Nutrient Film Technique (NFT). (For more information on this system, *see below* and Chapter 2.)

DIFFERENT METHODS OF HYDROPONICS

A number of growing methods come under the term hydroponics, such as the flood and drain method, drip feed, NFT, aeroponics and aquaponics. Construction details for a number of do-it-yourself systems demonstrated with drawings and photos are contained in Chapter 7. Alternatively, systems can be purchased by mail order or in person from suppliers.

The Flood and Drain Method

The flood and drain method provides the basics of hydroponics, performing very successfully all the tasks required by the roots of a plant.

A flood and drain system consists of a grow tray and a solution container connected together by a flexible pipe. The plants are placed in the grow tray, which has been filled with a mixture of sharp sand, perlite and baked clay balls. (Baked clay balls are marketed under a number of trade names and are produced by expanding special clay granules at over 2,192°F (1,200°C). Garden centres often use them to maintain moisture around the base of display plants.) The solution container is filled with a hydroponic mix of nutrient solution at the correct pH and strength for the plant being grown; this container is then raised above the grow tray to flood it. After giving the growing medium a good soaking, all the remaining solution is allowed to drain back fully into the solution container by placing it lower than the growing container, where it is then available for the next period of flood. As the solution is flooded in, unwanted gases around the roots are forced out, then as the solution drains out, air with the required oxygen is pulled in. This cycle leaves the roots of the plant fully supplied with every major and trace element it requires, along with a good ratio of air to nutrient solution.

Commercial plants are fed by drip feed into the top of the cube.

Drip Feed

The drip-feed method requires cubes of Rockwool, which are commercially available. These cubes (wrapped with plastic on the sides) are placed in contact with the Rockwool in the bolsters (looking like large growbags). A solution of nutrients and water is fed into the top of the cube containing the plant; it then flows down into the bolster and out into a collecting system. The solution is fed in at 25 per cent excess of the needs of the plants; in this way, the nutrient balance around the roots is maintained. This system is favoured by commercial growers.

Nutrient Film Technique

The NFT system can produce extremely good crops of tomatoes, using only a sheet of glass. The nutrient solution forms a thin film on the glass as it flows across it. The bare roots of the plant are then placed in this thin film and eventually the root mat will thicken. The plant grows with a fraction of the root mat in the solution, with the roots above being fed by capillary action from below.

Tomatoes growing on a sheet of glass.

A sheet of glass on the tray ready for the plant roots. Note also the green solution feed pipes.

When a plant is brought in, the medium it was growing in is removed.

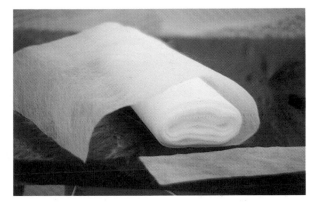

A roll of spreader mat.

Another NFT method is to use trays lined with or constructed of plastic. The nutrient solution is slowly fed on to the tray, the base of which is covered by a spreader mat that prevents the trickle of solution meandering down the tray and missing the bare roots of some of the plants. The solution then falls back into the tank at the end of the tray.

For further information on NFT, *see* Chapter 2.

Aeroponics

In this system, the plants' roots grow through a horizontal support and their roots are continually saturated with fine droplets of nutrient solution in a mist. Placing the roots of a plant into a solution and applying a very large number of small air bubbles into that solution can achieve a similar effect.

Aquaponics

A commercial system on these lines could produce tilapia fish. Tilapia has many strong culinary attributes. It has a mild, soft, white flesh with a slightly sweet taste. The meat is lean and the flakes are tender. Feeding the fish on duckweed, which happens to be very much at home in ponds or streams with high levels of organic matter, could produce a very commercially viable system.

The aquatic herb *lemnaceae* (duckweed is the common name) grows in fresh water, it is said to have the unique distinction of being the smallest flowering plant on earth. This plant is also unique in that it does not have any stem or leaf structures. The plant is simply a fleshy, flattened structure. These plants can double their mass in less than two days under ideal conditions of nutrient availability, sunlight and temperature. It has been calculated that a small patch of duckweed on the surface of a 1.235 acre (0.5 hectare) pond could possibly cover the entire surface in less than fifty days. It thrives on pollution.

A temperate pond (or container) containing tilapia fish and duckweed would be required, or a source of polluted water with duckweed in it; in this case the duckweed could be fed to the fish. The duckweed removes unwanted nutrients and waste products from the water, converting the nutrients into plant biomass. The plant biomass, in turn, becomes a high protein food for the tilapias. Within good systems the water is purified and conserved (recirculated); the fish are fed and a commercial product is produced.

It is said in a properly designed water recirculation and purification system, duckweed can remove as much as 99 per cent of the nutrients and dissolved solids in waste water.

COMMERCIAL GROWERS

In the 1970s the commercial world became very interested in hydroponics. Good, reliable growing methods capable of producing high-quality produce to supply the demands of the ever-increasing population were in demand. With the development of plastics, the success of hydroponics was assured. Before the introduction of plastics, systems had experienced problems due to the leaching of detrimental elements into the nutrient solution from the concrete and metals used in their construction. Fibreglass, plastic sheeting and plastic pipes solved this.

In 1979, Dr Allen Cooper, of the then Glasshouse Research Institute, designed a new growing system, NFT, and published his book on the subject. NFT was the first method of crop production that did not involve a solid rooting medium. Hydroponics now became very attractive to the commercial world. Enormous amounts of high-quality hydroponically grown products are produced around Europe commercially, including tomatoes, cucumbers, strawberries and lettuce. In Holland, tomatoes are raised in greenhouses that are known as 'glass cities', due to the large areas that they cover. The UK also grows vast amounts of tomatoes, cucumbers and lettuce using hydroponic methods, often in units that are very technologically advanced. The waste heat from Drax Power Station is used to supplement the high temperatures required by the huge areas of greenhouses owned by Geest PLC, which is one of the largest growers in the world, producing around 6,000 tons of tomatoes annually by hydroponic methods.

AMATEUR GROWERS

In the 1970s some amateur growers were also interested in hyrdroponics, but equipment and information were confined to the commercial grower at that time. Formulae were published in trade articles, but to make up the small amounts required would have involved costs beyond most amateur's means. Amateur growers therefore experimented with what was available to them. There were a number of proprietary brand powder fertilizers on the market, including Phostrogen, a dry powder mix of nutrients that is used as a general fertilizer after mixing with water. In the early 1970s it was used to make a hydroponic solution, with pea-sized gravel and sharp sand employed as the medium. The manufacturers of Phostrogen, when asked for further information, suggested adding boron and possibly extra chelated iron to the mix. The suggested method to add boron was to mix one level teaspoonful (5ml) of powdered borax to half a pint (280ml) of water. This was to be dissolved and twenty drops added to each 2gal (9l) of full-strength solution. Boron is now in the present mix. This mix served its purpose and gave reasonable results after experimenting with additions of chelated iron, calcium nitrate and the boron.

In the late 1970s the hydroponic mixes required became available to all growers in small quantities. The hydroponic mix, containing perfectly balanced nutrients, is now available by mail order from hydroponic suppliers. It can be bought as a powder in a two-pack mix or as a solution; both forms are very concentrated. Both are mixed with water and added to the system. The hydroponic mix of dry nutrients is supplied in the form of pack A and pack B. This is to overcome the problem of chemical precipitance (two or more useful salts joining to form something the plant cannot use or absorb) while in a concentrated form. The essential element calcium nitrate will react with other elements and so it is kept apart in pack A.

Growing Tomatoes

Tomato plants can be grown for a whole year on a sheet of glass. The roots will have formed a mat on

A root mat ready for disposal.

the glass around 1in (2.5cm) thick by the end of the year, after producing tomato crops of exceptionally high quality and in huge quantities.

Tomatoes that have ripened on a plant that has been fed with the correct balance of nutrients, at the correct strength and pH and without the presence of root pests, will be far superior to any of the same type grown in soil. A plant indulged in this way will also be better able to defend itself if pests attack the foliage.

As the solution (nutrients in water) is pumped round over and over again, automation of the system is easily achieved. With the addition of an easily made device, the nutrients in the solution can be replaced as the plants remove them, giving almost complete automation and leaving the grower to tend the tops of the plant, pick the produce and keep the greenhouse clean. The same unit can be used to add nutrients manually to the solution, maintaining the nutrient balance over a longer period without a solution change.

ORGANIC HYDROPONICS

The main material in hydroponics is water. Organic growers use a lot of this. Then there are the mineral elements. Most of these started out as mined rock or mineral deposits and as such are organic. If pests should attack, they can be controlled using their predators, enabling the grower to avoid the use of pesticides.

Two fully organic hydroponic systems use the water from an aquarium, a pond or even a fish

Tomatoes and watercress grown using pond water.

farm. Systems of this sort are especially good for plants like lettuce, which have a low demand for nutrients. Tomato plants have a high demand for nutrients, but the pond system can still be used. For example, the water from a pond with only ten gold-fish can produce large tomato plants and good crops of tomatoes, watercress or a vast display of flowers. Further details of this system of hydroponics can be found in Chapter 7. The fish in these systems also benefit considerably from a nutrient-free environment, as this starves the algae and enables the number of fish the pond is capable of supporting to be increased.

THE FUTURE

In the not too distant future, on space flights, plants and horticulture will play a very important part in the life of astronauts. Plants will have to provide food, as calories and amino acids, as well as converting carbon dioxide to oxygen. At the same time, the waste of both plants and humans will have to be converted into clean water and soluble nutrients. The treatment of this waste could possibly be carried out using a bio-reactor, and the resulting nutrient solution could feed the growing plants hydroponically. Given good light, plants can absorb up to four times the amount of carbon dioxide in fresh air. In the future, who can say where hydroponic systems will be found!

CHAPTER 2

Nutrient Film Technique

Dr Allen Cooper of the Glasshouse Research Institute in Sussex, England, originally designed the Nutrient Film Technique (NFT). In 1979 he published his book on the subject. He also did the first tests with Rupert Charlesworth of the British Agricultural Development and Advisory Service on supplying nutrients to plants as indicated by the cF. NFT is a closed, recirculating system.

An NFT system does not have a rooting medium. The plant is grown on a flat surface made from plastic, fibreglass or on a sheet of glass. It forms a root mat in a very shallow stream of recirculating solution. The nutrient solution must not come in contact with any metal – for instance, copper pipe could introduce copper at a toxic level.

The ideal situation for successful growth by NFT is that the nutrient solution is a film of consistent depth, usually about 0.125in (1–2mm), over the whole of a flat surface, with the root mat partly in and eventually partly above it. The root mat developing above the film of solution is in moist air, with a degree of capillary action from the film of solution below. NFT aims to supply all the needs of the plant's roots at all times. The plants require oxygen, moisture and warm solution (nutrient and water as food) in plenty around the roots. Around the leaves the environment should provide warm air (for the required carbon dioxide) and light in the correct spectrum.

Despite the many advantages of using the NFT system, there are some pitfalls that must be avoided. In conventional gardening, if the plants are watered to excess (waterlogged) the roots are starved of oxygen. If the soil dries out, then air containing oxygen penetrates the soil, but there is inadequate water. Similar imbalances can occur in NFT if the system design is poor, for example if there is a dip in the flat surface or if the slope on

that surface is incorrect. In these instances, pools of solution will form instead of a film and as the area of solution in contact with the air is reduced a drowned root system could result, as in a waterlogged garden. Forcing air through an air stone near the pump intake and introducing water cascades will help by increasing the oxygen content of the water at the point where the solution is introduced. If pools have formed or if the NFT tray is very long, then the oxygen content of the solution away from the source will be depreciated as the plants along the line take the oxygen. On the same basis, the inlet flow must not be so great as to form a considerable depth of solution. Nor should the slope be so acute that the flow washes the plants along. Too strong a flow of solution over the plant's roots can also prevent the plant taking up the nutrients it requires. The inlet flow to the flat surface and the gradient of the flat surface must be balanced.

Starting from Seed

The smallest amount of medium around the roots is the best for NFT. The seed can be started in very small cubes or pieces of Rockwool or small pots of Hortifibre.

Alternatively for NFT seed planting, a good mix of vermiculite and perlite allows the entire medium to be removed from the roots with minimum root damage.

Plants must not be placed on NFT trays until the root system is large enough.

Growing Tomatoes by NFT

The width of the channel should be wide enough to allow the roots to form without damming the

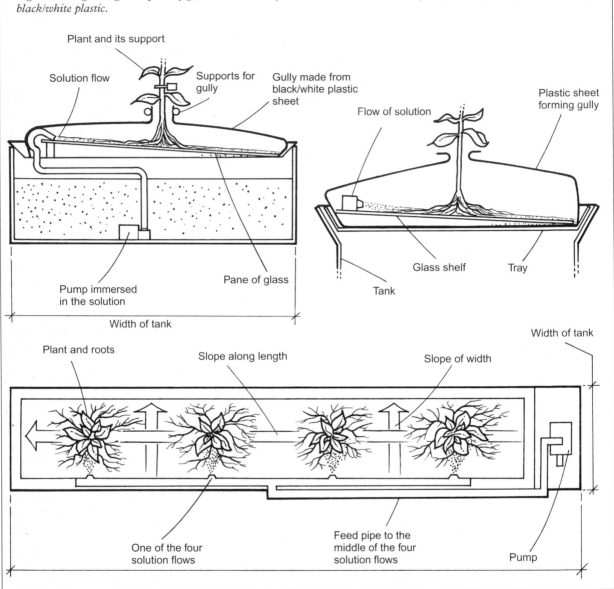

Fig 1. Plants growing on a pane of glass. The solution flows across and down the length of the tray. Gully is made out of black/white plastic.

Plant and its support

Solution flow

Supports for gully

Gully made from black/white plastic sheet

Plant and its support

Flow of solution

Plastic sheet forming gully

Pump immersed in the solution

Pane of glass

Width of tank

Glass shelf

Tray

Tank

Plant and roots

Slope along length

Slope of width

Width of tank

One of the four solution flows

Feed pipe to the middle of the four solution flows

Pump

solution. For tomatoes, spacing the plants around 12in (30cm) away from each other is ideal, although they have been successfully grown 7in (18cm) apart. Six tomato plants can be grown on the tray of one tank 14in × 5ft (35.5cm × 1.5m) for one full year without problems, but the foliage must be spread out above the tank to give the plants plenty of light and air. Removing the growing top of the plant and allowing only one truss of tomatoes per plant means tomatoes can be grown at a very high density, fourteen plants in an area 14in × 5ft (35.5cm × 1.5m). This gives the advantage of seed to clean-out time in two to three months. The root neck of some plants should be kept dry. Toma-

Plants in Hortifibre.

Seed grown in pieces of Rockwool.

Capsicums grown in perlite and vermiculite.

toes, however, will put out extra roots and so this is not a problem and it can be an advantage; laying the plant on its side will produce extra roots from the stem so increasing the root system.

Commercial growers often place six plants to a bolster and allow two stems to each root system, giving twelve plants to one bolster.

USING BLACK/WHITE PLASTIC TO FORM A GULLY OVER THE TRAY

This growing method uses black/white plastic folded in half along the width to make a gully; the black should be inside. The top of the gully (edges of the plastic) should be firmly attached to a strong support wire running above and parallel to the tray supporting the gully (clip-on clothes pegs are fine for this). Another wire above this one could support the plants until they are high enough to be supported from above by strings from the greenhouse roof. (*see* F in Fig 2). The black/white plastic must not be allowed to drop on to the roots (*see* C in Fig 2). It must allow the entry of air around the stem of the plant and along the gully; air must be able to reach the roots and circulate. In this way, any gases generated by the roots of the plants will be removed and at the same time a good supply of oxygen around the roots will be provided.

THE BLACK/WHITE GULLY SYSTEM

In each of these figures the arrows up from the nutrient represent the capillary action.

- **A** This is an end section of a correctly formed gully made out of black/white plastic sheeting.
- **B** This is an end section of a gully made using round-section guttering instead of square-section guttering, which results in the roots in the centre of the gully being in a pond when the root mat develops fully. They will then depend entirely on the oxygen in the solution flowing past them, as the nutrient is, of course, deeper and no longer a film. If the solution oxygen is low in the base of the gully, root death could take place.

- **C** This shows a distorted NFT gully made out of black/white plastic sheeting. The walls have been allowed to sag. The solid lines represent the walls of the badly supported black/white plastic sheeting forming the gully. The dotted tines represent the walls as they should be. The base of the gully is no longer flat and so a small pond has developed, giving a poor oxygen supply to the roots. The sagging walls are restricting the supply of fresh air to the roots, which could result in plant stress or even root death. If, in addition to this, the plastic is clipped tightly round the plant stem, then fresh air will not be able to get in at all, allowing diseases to attack the plant stem.

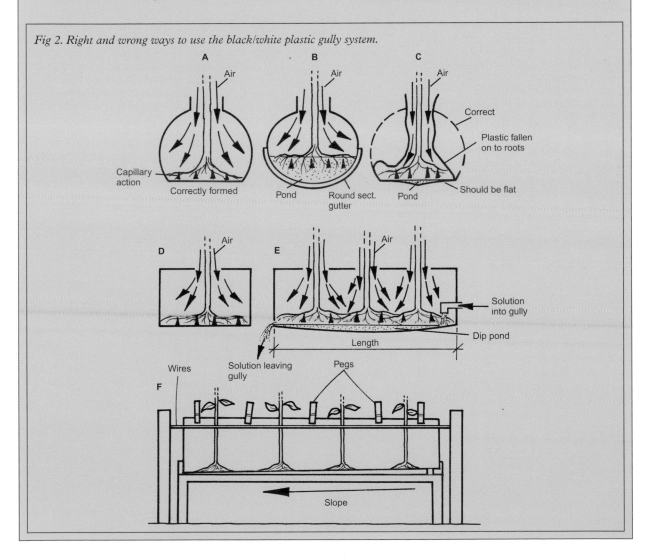

Fig 2. Right and wrong ways to use the black/white plastic gully system.

- **D** This shows a square section of gully, and provided it does not dip or pond along its length this is a well-formed system. However, the top will need to be a removable lid for each plant. A system with one lid can present problems, as removing that lid will result in all the plants in that run being lifted out, although if the planting holes are big enough then a fixed top may work all right.
- **E** Two parallel wires above a bench 1in (2.5cm) away from each other, support the black/white plastic sheeting that forms the gully. A dip exists in the middle of this length of gully; this could give a pond effect. Both of the top edges of the plastic sheeting forming the gully are clipped to these wires with clothes pegs. As the root system expands the plastic can be lowered to increase the base width. The grower is able to lower one side of the plastic sheeting to check on the state of the rooting system without disturbing the plants.
- **F** This is a drawing of the system in Figure E, showing two parallel wires above a bench about 1in (2.5cm) apart. The top edges of the black/white plastic sheeting are clipped on to them by clothes pegs, leaving a gap of 1in along the top of the length of the plastic sheeting. The bench has a good slope, is made of wood and has two sides. The two wires

Plants grown using black/white plastic to form a gully.

with the tops of the plastic sheeting attached will have the stems of the plants in-between them. Between the plants, clothes pegs hold the tops of the sheeting loosely together: this allows a good flow of air beside the stem of the plant. The bottom of the gully formed by the black/white plastic sheeting resting on the flat surface of the bench gives sufficient width for the gully to be expanded as the root system grows.

Small tomato plants growing in a black/white plastic gully.

THE FLOW RATE OF THE NUTRIENT SOLUTION

The flow rate of the nutrient solution should be around 0.22gal (1l) per minute for well-established plants, but around half of this for new plants. Very high flow rates should be avoided, as this can lead to flooding and cF problems (plants being unable to take up the nutrients due to the high flow rate).

The weight of the nutrient solution can be considerable, so a good firm foundation and insulation are required under the containers. The weight of the plants will be held from above. Some good bricks with wood and polystyrene slabs (as used in house insulation) on top would give the required

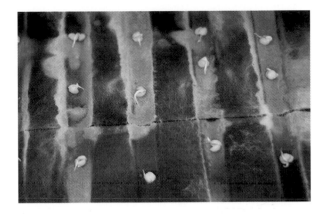

This shows edible peas on an NFT tray (the shell was removed when the taproot broke out).

Healthy peas; next stop, picking.

This shows the peas putting out adventurous roots over the spreader mat.

ADVANTAGES OF NFT

The advantages of the NFT system are considerable:

- the whole system can be fully automated except for the removal of shoots
- in a properly set-up system with a balanced feed and good environmental conditions, crops far exceeding other methods can be obtained
- NFT plants have a balanced diet presented to them, whereas in the soil a guarantee cannot be given that all the trace or major elements required are available
- there is no waste of water or nutrients, and no pollution. When a solution change is required, the spent solution can be beneficially used on soil-grown plants where the soil acts as a buffer. If facilities exist to have the solution analysed, the same solution can be used over and over again by adding the required nutrients, thus saving water
- lettuces grown in NFT can be removed from the system when ready, and if the roots are kept damp they will remain fresh for weeks
- tomatoes have a good shelf life when picked ripe
- tests have shown improved flavour (citric acid) and sugar content in hydroponic tomatoes compared to a plant of the same type grown in soil conditions
- no weeding.

DISADVANTAGES

Problems can occur due to:

- poor system design giving waterlogged conditions
- incorrect cF or pH of nutrient for the type of plant being grown
- breakdown of pumps or power supplies
- root infections in a system can spread (although this is also the case in soil).

Keeping to the requirements for NFT will solve the first two problems, but pumps and power supplies are another matter – a good reason for buying reliable pumps from a hydroponic supplier. Sensible hygiene precautions can prevent root infection.

support and insulation. The levels of the ground water should also be taken into consideration; early in the year; this can cool the system down.

Most crops such as cabbage (leafy crops), cucumbers, herbs, strawberries, sweet peppers, tomatoes, ornamental plants and flowers, even roses, will thrive in the NFT system. It can even be used for orchids if a very low cF is used.

CHAPTER 3

The Solution: Major and Minor Nutrients

Plants need the same nutrients whether grown in soil or hydroponically. In soil, the elements are provided by organic material decomposing and hopefully producing the required elements. In hydroponics, the grower creates a suitable environment for the foliage and provides all the required elements by means of the nutrient solution. The strength or concentration of the nutrients in the solution is measured as cF units.

OSMOSIS

The roots of a plant are composed of small cells, and by the process of osmosis (that is, a different strength of salts on the outside of the cells compared to that on the inside of the cells) the plant takes up nutrients and water. Water or a very weak solution (low cF) on the outside of these cells will enable the plant to absorb the maximum amount of water or water with nutrients. Equally, a very concentrated solution (very high cF) will make the strength of the solution higher on the outside of the cells compared to that inside, and so the flow will be from the plant roots to the solution, which would result in plants which do not thrive. This will occur either in conventional growing or in hydroponics. The cF of the solution must be matched to the type of plant and the sort of growth required. If a plant is looking droopy and yet appears to be well watered (not drowned), then it could be that the plant roots are being attacked or the concentration of salts around the roots is far too high.

THE NUTRIENT SOLUTION

In the concentrated nutrient packs obtainable from hydroponic suppliers, calcium nitrate and

POTENTIAL VOLTAGES ON ROOTS

An article by Eugene Diatloff entitled 'Riddle of the Roots' appeared in the September/October 1993 issue of the magazine *Practical Hydroponics & Greenhouses International*. This article goes into great detail on the make-up of plant roots. For instance, the root of the plant is able to absorb selectively nutrients using energy in the root cells to maintain an electro-chemical potential difference of around 120mV negative to 180mV negative across the plasma membrane. Positively charged nutrients such as potassium (K^+) and calcium (Ca_2^+) are attracted by a negative charge, while phosphate ($H_2PO_4^-$) requires additional energy to get across the membrane to overcome being repelled by the internal negative charge. The roots of the plant are receiving a lot of attention from science, and rightly so, as it is a very important area of study.

As long as the nutrients are supplied in the correct balance and at the correct pH from the start, then the plants are able to be selective, that is within a normal cF range, say cF5 to cF28, depending on plant type and size.

TAKING THE SOLUTION FROM A HIGH cF TO WATER

Going from a high cF feed to plain water will in itself introduce shock to the plants so care must be taken. Do not flush with plain water, flush if necessary using a weak solution.

COMMERCIAL GROWERS USE cF AS A CONTROL

In commercial hydroponics, the grower often boosts up the cF from normal to achieve different effects. In poor light conditions such as midwinter, tomato plants can become 'leggy', but by feeding a high cF the uptake of solution and nutrients is inhibited, thereby slowing growth. When the light improves, the cF is returned to normal. The cost of providing plants with high-intensity light over such large areas would not be cost-effective.

magnesium will react together, so they are kept apart. Precipitation (two or more useful salts joining to form something the plant cannot use or absorb) can result in essential elements forming ingredients, such as plaster of Paris, which cannot be absorbed or appreciated by plants. To overcome this problem, the powder nutrients are supplied in two packs, pack A and pack B. Pack A will have the calcium nitrate and in some mixes part of the iron, while pack B will contain the rest of the main elements along with the trace elements. The nutrient solution can also be obtained in a combined liquid form.

The two-pack dry mixes should be thoroughly mixed with the quantity of water recommended by the supplier in two separate containers. It is not recommended to mix part now and the rest later as some elements are in such small quantities that the mixes could become unbalanced. As long as the mixes are kept away from any light source, they will keep for a year. Both should be mixed well again before use. Each time the cF falls below the current value it is then a simple matter to add, say, Xml of A, stir the solution to mix, then add Xml of B and stir again.

Extra care is required when combining concentrated mixes of A and B to make the original solution. During this operation comparatively large amounts of concentrated solution are being added to the main tank. The solution should be well agitated before and after adding the second mix.

The two-part mix enables the grower to increase the nitrogen content of the solution by adding extra of mix A. This would be for foliage plants like lettuce or cabbage. For growing lettuce, adjusting the levels of calcium to potassium ratio can overcome the problem of leaf-tip burn when there is a low cF (cF10 or just below). For tomatoes, a higher cF will give better results for mature plants. For further information, *see* the guide to cF values for each plant at the end of this chapter.

While the solution can be made up at home – the basic formula is not a secret – it is far cheaper and easier to buy the powder as mix A and mix B, or as a single pack of concentrated solution. To make a mix for 44 pints (25l) of water would require a scale that could read portions of a gram. To buy the chemicals needed in the small quantities required

CHANGING THE BALANCE OF A TO B FOR THE FLOWERING STAGE OF GROWTH

The balance between A and B can be altered when the plant comes to the flowering stage. Extra of B will increase the potassium and phosphorus for the flowering stage. However, the balance of nutrients in the original mix A or mix B should not be altered. High potassium/phosphorus solution can be given for flowers (Pack B), and high nitrogen for leaves (Pack A).

However, the A and B mixes can be obtained as bloom mixes, which is a safer way. When a plant produces flowers, the plant takes up more potassium and less nitrogen. Grow and bloom formulations are available in the two part or single mixes. If the grower does not want to experiment (which should be done with caution, as damage can occur) with the levels of A and B applied to the solution, then the bloom mixes are the answer.

would be extremely expensive. The mix should contain as many chelated compounds as possible. They are less liable to react with other elements at the higher pH values and are more water-soluble. Iron chelates assure iron is available to the plants at higher pH ranges. Even so, aim for a mix with the potential Hydrogen adjusted to pH6.

THE MAJOR AND MINOR ELEMENTS

In total, plants require sixteen elements in significant amounts, plus many more elements in minute amounts. Many of the latter are present in the plant's environment and so can be ignored in hydroponics. Of the sixteen essential elements, the air and the environment around the plant supply three of these. They are oxygen, carbon and hydrogen. Photosynthesis takes place in the plant leaves, converting the sunlight (or artificial light) energy into carbohydrates using these three elements.

The remaining thirteen elements support the photosynthesis process either directly or in other ways. Six of the thirteen elements are required in large amounts and are known as major elements. These are nitrogen, potassium, phosphorus, calcium, magnesium and sulphur. Potassium and phosphorus are taken up in greater quantity in low light, while in strong light nitrogen is taken up in greater quantity.

The remaining seven are minor or trace elements: iron, manganese, copper, zinc, boron, molybdenum and chlorine. Iron can turn into rust if the pH conditions are not right, resulting in a loss of iron to the plants.

Around 35 per cent of the dry weight of a plant is composed of carbon. If the carbon dioxide levels in a greenhouse can be increased during periods of light, the plants will benefit. (It is not recommended doing this in the house, as high levels are harmful to us.) Up to four times the level of carbon dioxide found in fresh air can be beneficial for plant growth, but only when the plants are exposed to sunlight (or artificial light). The carbon dioxide would need to be provided in bottled form; do not attempt to obtain it by burning fossil fuels.

Chlorine exists in most piped water supplies and like all trace elements can be toxic if applied in excess of the required quantity. Chlorine can be used to disinfect the system.

Copper piping or any metal in the plumbing must be kept well away from contact with the mixed solution. Copper or a metal could be absorbed by the solution at a toxic level. Copper piping should be used for water feed only. Polypropylene is a good material for all fittings and piping in contact with the mixed solution, as it is non-toxic to plants. Black absorbs heat and stands up to UV light better.

CLOSED SYSTEM MANAGEMENT

When using a closed system where the bulk of the nutrient is pumped round the system continually (recycled), two methods can be adopted for nutrient management. The first does not require a cF meter at all. Using the commercial two-part mixes, pack A and pack B, the two packs of dry powder are made up into two containers in a concentrated form using the quantities of water recommended by the supplier. Each time these concentrated mixes are used, mix well beforehand. The two solutions are then labelled A and B and kept apart in this concentrated form in a light-free area. An equal quantity of each concentrated mix (as recommended by the supplier) is then added to 1gal (4.5l) of water to give a set cF value. This solution is then placed in the main tank. If this method is adopted then the size of the main tank will dictate how often the solution is changed. For instance, if the tank holds 30gal (136l) of solution, when 30gal of solution at the correct cF has been used to top up the main tank, the remaining solution should be replaced with a new mix.

In the second method, the solution strength is maintained either using a homemade cF meter or one from a hydroponic supplier. Both solutions should be mixed as in the first method, then Xml of concentrated mix A is added to the water in the main tank. The solution should be agitated to mix, then the same amount (Xml) of B is added. A further agitation of both A and B will be necessary before a true reading can be taken. The solution must be the same temperature each time a reading is taken, unless the meter has a temperature compensation facility. Once mixed up in a weak solution, reaction between the elements is reduced. This method allows the solution to be used for longer periods. If the solution is submitted for analysis to a laboratory (hydroponics suppliers can recommend suitable laboratories for this) and only the elements required to maintain the balance are added, the water can be used over and over. The pH is adjusted to match the type of plant being grown.

Using a cF Test Solution

For perfect results, buy a commercial hydroponic cF test solution from a hydroponic supplier. The test solution is usually sold as 2.76 mS/cm (microsiemens per centimetre), which is the same as cF27.6 at 77°F (25°C). This must be stored out of direct sunlight in a cool place and brought up to the temperature of 77°F (25°C) before using to test. An exception to this is when using a cF meter with temperature compensation.

CONDUCTIVITY

The nutrient supplied as indicated by a cF meter and the appearance of the plants will be enough to

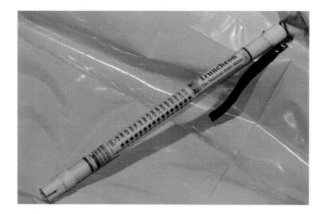

New Zealand Truncheon (cF meter).

grow a satisfactory crop of tomatoes at home. However, in the modern commercial world of hydroponics, sensors in the solution feed-lines to the plants pass the required information to computers, which control the pH and the nutrients fed to the plants. The grower uses the experience gained by growing a particular crop to control the computer.

A reading given by an Electrical Conductivity (EC) meter gives the strength of the nutrient. The meter can give a reading as cF (conductive Factor), EC (Electrical Conductivity) or ppm (parts per million), or all three. The New Zealand Truncheon nutrient salts meter is calibrated in all three readings. A reading of cF2 is the same as 0.2 EC and the same as 140ppm. Readings given by cF meters indicate the total concentration of the mix of nutrients in a solution, *not the individual nutrient components*.

Using a cF Meter

A cF meter cannot tell what sorts of salts are in the solution, only how much in total, and so a value of cF always refers to a particular mix of nutrients. To compare one mix of nutrients with another, both mixes must contain exactly the same balance of nutrients and must be at the same temperature. The cF reading can then tell the grower which is the strongest mix.

When tap water or well water with a high base conductivity (water already containing a lot of salts) is used to mix the solution and a recirculating system is used, then frequent changes of the

---

HOW THE cF, EC VALUE IS OBTAINED

The cF of the solution is derived by applying an AC voltage across two electrodes immersed in the solution, resulting in an alternating electric current flowing between the electrodes. It must be an alternating current flowing across the electrodes or one electrode or the other may change its connection with the solution over time due to a form of electroplating. The current flow in the circuit will depend upon the AC voltage applied and the electrical resistance of the solution. An AC voltage (12V) applied to the probes (electrodes) with a suitable meter and a bridge rectifier in the circuit will enable the DC current flowing in the circuit to be measured. Using Ohms law and substituting the known values:

$$R = \frac{E}{I}$$. In the formula R is in ohms, E is in volts and I is in amps.

The solution current can be measured and converted into electrical resistance R and then into conductance (G).

Electrical conductance (G) is the reciprocal of the resistance R.

$$G = \frac{1}{R}$$.

The inverse of the spelling ohm gives mho, which is the unit previously used for electrical conductance (G).

However, the new international unit for electrical conductance (G) is siemens (S); the unit for electrical conductivity is siemen/metre. The siemen/metre is too large a unit for our use and so the electrical conductivity is given in decisiemens/metre (dS/m): 1dS/m = cF10.

As a matter of interest, the electrical conductance (EC) units having the same value are: 100mS/m = 1dS/m = 1mS/cm = 1000µS/cm = cF10 = 1m/mho.

- 1ml of water weighs 1g.
- One part per million (ppm) is 1g in 1,000,000g.
- One part per million (ppm) is 1g (or 1ml) in 1,000l of distilled water.
- TDS (Total Dissolved Solids) is proportional to conductivity in mmho for a unit volume and is expressed in mg/l.

solution are required, possibly every two to three weeks, instead of six to seven weeks when using a very low base cF solution. This is because any salts in the water that are not required, or are not taken up by the plants, will get progressively stronger as the plants absorb the required nutrients. The system will continue to add more water complete with more unwanted salts. Eventually, the amount of unwanted salts will become too great, and the solution will need to be analysed or changed.

Water in its pure state is an insulator, that is if pure water could actually be obtained. When ionically bonded compounds like salt (NaCl) are added to water they dissociate (break up) into their constituent positively and negatively charged ions (Na^+ and Cl^-). This process causes water to become a better conductor. The degree of conductivity depends on the type of ions present in the solution, their concentration and the temperature of the solution. The approximate rate of variation with temperature is 2 per cent per degree Celsius. The electrical conductivity of a solution increases with temperature. Therefore, if the EC of the solution can be measured and the temperature of the solution is known, the value of the EC can be used to determine the concentration of the nutrient in the solution. The standard temperature for EC measurement is 77°F (25°C), and so to have a correct EC or cF reading, the solution must be at 77°F (25°C) or a correction made.

To find the base conductivity of the water, a reading should be taken in a litre of distilled water and then compared to the reading taken in a litre of water that is being used. Then, if it is a homemade cF meter, both these readings should be compared with a solution of a known strength.

All cF meters must be tested at regular intervals and the probe tip cleaned (if it is graphite) with very fine wet and dry paper. The instructions for maintenance supplied by the manufacturer should be followed.

THE EFFECT OF PH ON THE SOLUTION AND PLANTS

The pH is important both in conventional growing and in hydroponics. In hydroponics, the aim is to

---

A USEFUL LIST OF cF VALUES FOR DIFFERENT PLANTS

All the cF values here are given as a guide for well-established mature plants and for hydroponic mixes.

- African violets require a cF of 10 to 12.
- Asparagus requires a cF of 15 to 17 with a deep container.
- Balm, basil, borage, fennel, lavender, mint, sage and thyme require a cF of 12 to 16.
- Beans, beetroot, broccoli, Brussels sprouts, cabbage, cauliflower, chives, melons, parsnip, radish, roses, spinach, strawberries and turnip all require a cF of 18 to 24 (beetroot, radish, turnip and parsnip should be in sand and gravel).
- Peas require a cF of 14 to 19.
- Peppers and tomatoes require a cF of 20 to 29.
- Parsley and watercress require a cF of 5 to 16.
- Lettuce requires a low cF, around 4 to 10.
- Mustard and cress require a cF of 12 to 25.
- Onions require a cF of 18 to 24.

If the cF values are being used for soil-grown plants, the above cF values are, of course, for complete mixes of hydroponic nutrients and not for individual salts.

---

have a medium in which the solution pH can be controlled between 5.8 and 6.5. In conventional growing, the soil acts as a buffer on the pH, tending to keep it at a certain value. This, depending upon the type of soil and the plant being grown, can be a problem. A pH of 6.5 is the best in soil for availability of nutrients, but in hydroponics pH6 is the best.

The pH can directly affect the availability of nutrients to the plants. Precipitation can be caused in different degrees by the pH. At pH extremes certain nutrients become unavailable altogether to the plants and others change form. It can also have a big effect on the ability of the roots to assimilate nutrients.

The leaves of a plant will indicate whether there is any deficiency, but normally it is too late by then. Iron and magnesium deficiencies show via the leaves. Iron in the solution in a chelated form can help to overcome iron deficiency. At a very high pH (above pH8), iron in the solution ceases to exist due to iron hydroxide precipitation.

CHANGING THE PH OF A SOLUTION

Adjustments to the pH are made with acids or alkalis. Great care should be taken when working with any acid, but especially so with nitric acid, as it is a hazardous material to work with. ***Acid should always be added to water, never water to acid as it can explode.*** Nitric acid can be used to lower the pH, but it also increases the nitrates. Phosphoric acid increases the phosphate, although it requires much more to have the same effect on the pH. When ordering nutrients, it must be stated whether the water to be used is hard or soft. In this way, the phosphate level in mix B can be adjusted. Water with a very high pH (hard water) will need more acid, which will lead to an increase in the phosphate level over time when recirculating the solution. This can inhibit the uptake of zinc and other elements.

The pH should be checked and adjusted as the plants are growing, but any big changes should not be made over a short period of time. It is very easy to add too much acid. Adjust the pH in the top-up water tank (if used) as well. The change will be slow at first, then as the buffer of the solution goes the pH reading will quickly drop. Small amounts of phosphoric acid are added to lower the pH and bicarbonate or potassium hydroxide to raise the pH. Suppliers sell 'pH up' and 'pH down'.

As a very rough guide, around 1ml of phosphoric acid will lower 9gal (41l) of solution from pH7 to pH6, but this will depend on the type and quality of the water (soft or hard).

Root damage can take place at very low pH levels. Above pH6.8 precipitation can take place with some elements like iron, calcium and phosphorus.

THE pH CAN CHANGE BETWEEN NIGHT AND DAY

With well-established plants, the pH of a solution can vary considerably, even between daylight and dark periods of a day. The pH reading should therefore be taken at the same time each day. This will save adding 'pH up' then 'pH down' when not really necessary. Aim for pH5.8 to pH6.5. Below pH5.7, calcium and manganese become less soluble. Aluminium, which can become toxic if it is made available at too high a value, is more soluble below pH5.7.

At pH values above 7.6, manganese, zinc, iron, copper and boron are not so available to the roots.

Calcium acts like a glue to keep the cells of the plant together. Lack of it affects the extremities of the plant. In the case of tomatoes, the part of the fruit away from the plant turns black (black bottom); in lettuces, the extreme edges of the leaves turn brown (tip burn).

A pH pen is an electronic pH-testing device with a liquid crystal display. While very useful, it is rather expensive at around £50. Aquarium pH test kits sold by aquarium stores are very simple and cheap to use, but are somewhat messier. Hydroponic suppliers sell kits to test the pH; these are both effective and cheap. Usually a drop of a liquid (supplied with the kit) is added to a sample of the solution and the colour compared with a chart. Comparing the colour of the test solution with a colour chart from a hydroponic supplier can give accurate readings over a wide range.

Liquid silicon can be added to the solution to raise the pH. Dilute in fresh clean water first and add in very small amounts. Silicon added in the correct amounts (follow the manufacturer's detailed instructions) improves the uptake of nutrients, strengthens cell walls (which helps plants resist fungi and mites), increases chlorophyll production (giving darker green leaves), increases uptake of available CO_2 and adds extra potassium to support export flowering. Silicon cannot be added to the concentrated mixes at the manufacturing stage because it is so alkaline.

DEFICIENCIES

Deficiencies will not be experienced if:

- the pH is kept under control
- the A and B concentrated nutrients are hydroponic mixes
- the solution is stirred properly between adding A and B concentrates
- the cF and the flow of solution are correct for the size and type of plant
- a good environment is maintained.

The environment is of course very important; light affects the uptake of nitrogen, potassium and phosphorus. Some modern one-part hydroponic mixes such as 'Ionic' are especially good at holding the pH steady.

The causes of some problems that could be experienced with hydroponics are:

- over-fertilization (cF too high)
- under-fertilization (cF too low)
- low light or light period too short
- incorrect colour spectrum of artificial light
- cold air or cold solution.

DEFICIENCIES AND PROBLEMS IN TOMATO PLANTS

Magnesium Deficiency
- This shows as intervening yellowing and browning of the lower leaves. The solution should be changed.

Manganese Deficiency
- A low level can give a leaf-mottling effect; alternatively, if the level is too high there will be brownish lesions on the stems or blue-black colouration on the leaf tips, with the plant drooping.
- High and low levels of iron can have an effect on the availability of manganese.

Iron Deficiency
- This shows as yellowish blanching with bright green veins. The cF is too high or the pH is incorrect.

Tips of Leaves Burnt
- This is caused by damaged roots, resulting in poor calcium uptake. The most likely reason is that the root system was too small when placed in the system. Reduce the cF. If the plant is very small, take it out of the system and feed it on a very low cF (cF2 or 3) in good light until the root ball is bigger.
- Highly toxic gases from burnt fossil fuels can also give this effect.

Nitrogen Too High or Too Low
- High levels can give lush growth in lots of plants but reduce flowering.
- If the nitrogen is low, the lower leaves will be yellow.
- Take-up is related to the light intensity – either too intense or not enough!

Phosphorus Deficiency
- This affects root development. Shortage gives a colouration on the underside of the leaf. When soft water is used, less phosphoric acid is required to control the pH; it may be necessary to add extra phosphate to the nutrient solution to compensate for this. It should be stated when ordering nutrients if the water is soft or hard.

Potash Deficiency
- A shortage gives marginal leaf scorch; an excess gives stunted blue-tinted growth and can lead to burning of leaf tips. Take-up is light-intensity related.

Splits in Fruit
- Splits on the tomato fruits could be the result of low levels of copper or boron.

Curling Leaves
- If the tomato leaves curl down their length, this could be due to too high a contrast between day and night temperatures.

Yellow Old Leaves
- This could be the result of potassium, nitrogen, magnesium deficiency, or just old age!

Yellow or Brown Spots on Leaves
- Yellow or brown spots on leaves could be the result of either too cold water or fluoride toxicity.

Plan for prevention, not cure. If the A and B nutrients are given every attention along with the pH and the environment, then deficiency troubles will not occur.

CHAPTER 4

The Roots, Oxygen and Heat

OXYGEN AND ROOTS

Oxygen is very important to the roots of all plants. Water cascading, air pumps forcing air through an air stone producing lots of small bubbles, rain falling through the air and the surface area of solution in contact with the air, all affect the oxygen content of the solution. Rain will not affect systems in a greenhouse, but should be taken into account for systems placed outside; the cF may be diluted as well as the oxygen content being increased. When covers are placed over the root mass to prevent algae growing, provision should be made for air to enter around the neck of each plant. Algae consume nutrients and could be a home for pests. Hygiene is also extremely important when moving between soil plants and hydroponic plants, especially composts and contaminated plants. Fungal diseases prefer values of pH3 to pH5 with the temperature above 79°F (26°C). Remove any decayed material from around the system.

ROOT DAMAGE

Healthy roots are white. There are various ways in which roots can be damaged.

- If solution temperatures rise above 82°F (28°C), this puts stress on tomato plants. Between 68°F and 77°F (20°C and 25°C) are the best temperature settings for the solubility of nutrients.
- Solution temperatures can fall towards the end of the run; if the temperature falls too low, for example below 57°F (14°C) for tomatoes, root damage will occur.
- The roots should not be allowed to dry out.
- At the end of a trough of plants when it is a long run or if flooding (ponding or pools) occurs, the oxygen supply around the roots can become too low.
- Rough handling of plants can result in root damage.
- If pesticides get into the solution, this can also adversely affect the roots. If the foliage is sprayed with pesticide, take precautions to prevent any excess coming into contact with the roots and the solution. If the plants must be sprayed arrange to do so before a solution change.

Healthy white roots.

THE GROWING MEDIA

The function of the hydroponic media (as noted below, not used in NFT except for starting seedlings) is to give support to the plants, and to ensure that oxygen and water are readily available around the roots while at the same time giving good drainage. Some media have good capillary capacity (water will soak up from the base); others have to be fed from the top so that the solution will flow down through them. All media used in hydroponics must be inherently void of any nutrients and must not affect any of the nutrients applied to them. The pH of the solution in any medium should be fully controllable. When the solution has been applied and the excess has drained off, the ideal ratio would be around 40 per cent air to 60 per cent solution.

Various media can be utilized in a flood and drain recirculating system. They will react in different ways.

Coarse Sand

Fine sand tends to clog, with poor air-to-solution ratio. Coarse washed river sand around 0.08in (2mm) behaves well.

Gravel

This is best mixed with coarse sand. Any gravel with an alkaline nature must be avoided, as this tends to cause problems with high pH and iron.

Hortifibre, Coarse Sawdust and Straw

These are very good for short-term crops. In flood and drain, over a long period of time a degree of composting will take place, resulting in a loss of nitrogen and a bad air-to-solution ratio. Hortifibre simulates the orchid's natural environment, and is suitable for a flood and drain system.

Perlite

This is very good. The pH is easy to control; it does not contain any nutrients and has a very good capillary action. Perlite tends to float and depending upon the system used can give problems with filters.

Porous Clay Balls

Clay is fired in rotary kilns to form balls of porous clay of different sizes. This medium is very good for indoor plants. However, in flood and drain systems, if the plants have fine roots then movement of the clay balls can do damage unless they are held down.

Pumice

This is good, but, like perlite, small particles float around. Its capillary action is poor compared with that of perlite.

Rockwool

This is an excellent medium and is used extensively in commercial systems. Please note that rock wool as used in house insulation is of no use as a hydroponic medium as it will have been treated to prevent pests and has a different structure. Hydroponic Rockwool usually comes in slab or block form with the grain running from top to bottom. Over 90 per cent of the pore space is available for solution retention, giving it a very good air-to-solution ratio. The pH can be controlled easily, making it a good all-round media. Commercial growers favour drip-feed systems in Rockwool. Using flood and drain, Rockwool can simulate an orchid's natural environment.

Vermiculite

This inorganic material is very lightweight. It is made by heating flaked and fragmented mica to very high temperatures, so that it is able to hold large volumes of solution or water. Mica contains magnesium, potassium and aluminium. However, vermiculite can eventually lose its structure (not holding sufficient air), and other media may have to be mixed with it. Once vermiculite has been used and is wet, moving it around can cause it to compact and lose its formation. When used to plant seeds for NFT, it only needs to be used for a short time and is very easy to remove from the roots before placing the plants on the glass/plastic trays.

LIGHT AND HEAT IN HYDROPONICS

Hydroponically grown plants require the same attention and conditions (light, heat and air) as soil-grown crops. The colour of the light is important. Plants use the same range of colours as the human eye, but are more sensitive and react more to the violet/blue and orange/red spectrum. The green/yellow portion of the spectrum tends to be reflected; this is why the leaves are seen as green. The prime pigment of photosynthesis is chlorophyll. Chlorophyll-a is very active on blue 430 nanometres (nm) and red 660nm, while chlorophyll-b is active on blue 460nm and orange 640nm. Carotene (carotenoids, orange-yellow pigments) are active around 400nm to 500nm. A special meter is available that when used with colour filters can give an equal response to any colour between 400nm, the wavelength of violet light, and 720nm, the wavelength of red light. Using a basic module with a light-dependent resistor (LDR) as the sensor but without the relay, the lamp and the timer fitted can give extremely interesting readings for the intensity of light at a fixed point. Filters

(gelatine photographic filters) can be placed between the light source and the LDR when it is hand-held. A light meter sold for photographic use will give an indication of the intensity of light falling on a leaf.

The module used in this way and modified as in Fig 3, without any connections to pins 1 and 7, will give a reading, which will show the relative value of light falling on a point. *See* Chapter 8 for further details.

Plants require light of sufficient intensity for a good part of the day, but also require a period of darkness. Tomatoes, for instance, require a seven-hour period of darkness. The take-up of some nutrients is directly related to the light available. A large selection of lighting units for both indoor growing areas and greenhouse systems is available from the hydroponic supplier Growell.

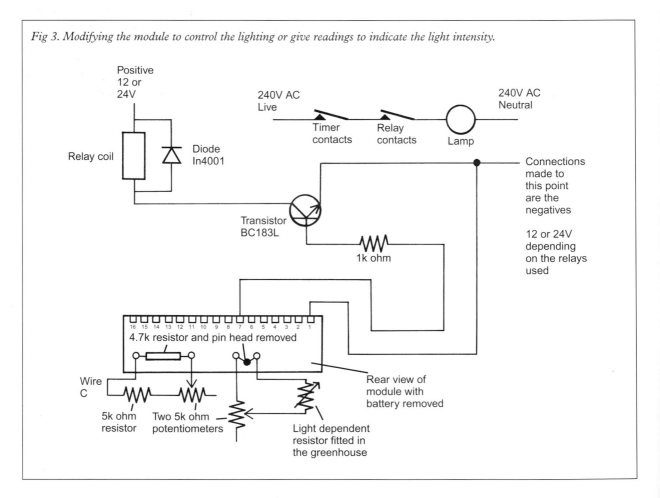

Fig 3. Modifying the module to control the lighting or give readings to indicate the light intensity.

CONTROL OF MAINS-OPERATED EQUIPMENT BY UNITS GIVING OUT 1.5V DC

Figure 14 (*see* page 65) is used in all the circuits in this book involving the control of mains-operated equipment. It converts the 1.5V DC positive given by the module into 240V AC. When 1.5V DC positive from the module (or any source) is applied to the base of a correct type of transistor via a 1k ohm resistor it switches it into the 'on state', current flows through the transistor, the relay coil and the relay contacts operate. The 240V AC live connected to one side of the relay contacts is switched on to the appliance, which has 240V AC neutral on its other terminal. Current now flows through the equipment operating it.

The construction of Fig 14 can be as an integrated circuit (IC) or made up in this form.

300W GLASS TUBE HEATERS

Immersing the glass tube heater in the solution results in hard scales of salts being baked on to the outside of the glass after a year of use. The scale is best removed at clean-out time, although it can be avoided altogether by fully immersing the heater in a container (with a depth greater than that of the solution) of clean water (no nutrient). The container, heater and clean water are then placed in the solution where the heater will perform its duties by conduction without being in direct contact with the solution. However, the clean water in the container must be kept topped up above the glass tube of the heater or it will crack. Position this container (with the clean water and the heater in) so that it receives any automatic top-up water for the main tank.

Heat and Root Growth

The temperature around the leaves and roots is, of course, important. The best air temperatures around the leaves for tomatoes in a greenhouse are 61°F (16°C) for night and 66°F (19°C) for day, ventilating at around 77°F (25°C). Heating the solution to 77°F (25°C) (the optimum temperature for tomatoes and peppers) using a 300W glass tube heater will give better root growth. With solution heating, the night air temperature around tomatoes can be reduced to 50°F (10°C) and even lower.

CHAPTER 5

Units Suitable for a Greenhouse

GREENHOUSE WALL UNIT

A wall unit constructed from house guttering (forming an NFT system), and attached to the side of an 8ft × 6ft (2.44m × 1.83m) or a similar greenhouse could give a considerable increase in the growing space available. This unit would consist of square-section house guttering arranged on both long walls of the greenhouse in the form of a 'V' on its side. The end wall of the greenhouse would have a solution tank in the middle at a level below the lowest point of the 'V'. The solution would be pumped up by an immersible pump positioned in the main tank to the highest points of both lengths of guttering attached to both sides of the greenhouse. The solution will then run down the top guttering on the north side and the top guttering on the south side until it comes to the down-comer section. At this point it will fall into the lower sections of both lengths of house guttering (on both sides of the greenhouse), and the solution from

The healthy roots in the greenhouse guttering unit.

both sides will be channelled into the main tank in the middle of the end wall. As long as the pump is running the solution will be circulated round both systems in the greenhouse. If a hydroponic solution is now put in the tank and a spreader mat is placed on the base of all the lengths of guttering to stop the solution meandering down, then when the plants with the bare roots are put in position they will grow. (*See* Fig 19 on page 80, which demonstrates the principle of a unit that can be used both on the walls of greenhouses and as a flower display in place of hanging baskets.) The space in the centre of the greenhouse could either be left empty, or it could have some small flood and drain hydroponic plant pots on a narrow bench down the middle. If enough space is available in the centre between the two 'V' formations, then a unit as shown in Fig 4 could be placed in the middle.

A number of lengths of guttering can be placed alongside each other on a table or bench. When the bench is arranged with a good slope, the solution pumped up to the top of all the channels will run down them in parallel. At the bottom, the solution will be collected and returned to the main tank containing the pump. The number of channels will depend on the space available. A system like this can be constructed or purchased from a hydroponic supplier. A unit such as this can be placed in a greenhouse, on a patio or veranda – in fact anywhere with good light and heat.

Nutriculture Ltd, a hydroponic supplier, makes Gro-Tanks in a number of sizes; these can be purchased from most suppliers. A number of these tanks could be positioned along both sides of the greenhouse or in any free area with warmth and good light. A Gro-Tank kit is a good starting point for the novice hydroponic grower. They can be

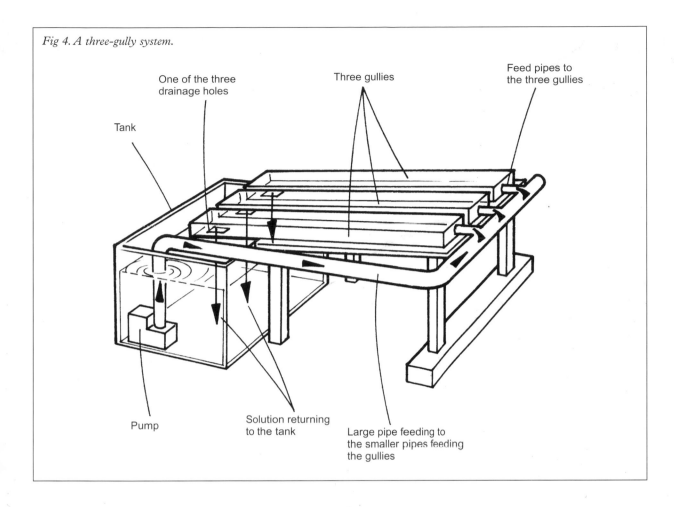

Fig 4. A three-gully system.

One of the three drainage holes

Three gullies

Feed pipes to the three gullies

Tank

Pump

Solution returning to the tank

Large pipe feeding to the smaller pipes feeding the gullies

ordered as complete kits. Everything required is provided – a small quantity of phosphoric acid, a spreader mat, a pump, a dry mix of hydroponic nutrient and a Gro-Tank. All the grower need state is the size of the unit required and whether the water to be used is hard or soft. Strawberries, tomatoes, peppers, lettuce, melons, even cucumbers, can be grown using this equipment, although it must be remembered that the environment around the plant foliage must be correct. Hydroponics enables the grower to get the best from the plant by providing its roots with everything it requires. It is up to the grower to do the same for the foliage.

A cF meter is well worth having but not essential. Without one, the solution should be changed at intervals to prevent the nutrients becoming out of balance. A pH pen is also useful, but again not

essential. The pH can be tested with a colour comparison chart.

CHOOSING THE RIGHT SYSTEM

The grower will get the best results if he or she knows a little about the plant itself and its general requirements, such as whether it likes acid conditions (low pH), strong light, sheltered spots and so on. The most suitable hydroponic system should be chosen for the plant being grown. For example, if it is a root vegetable, flower bulb, rose or fig tree, the best system would be flood and drain in a media such as coarse sand. For plants such as tomatoes, peppers, melons and cucumbers, then the best system would be NFT.

Seedling trees can be grown using hydroponics, making it possible to achieve larger numbers per area than could be grown in the same area of soil. The seed germination and root systems are better due to the supply of a balanced nutrient solution with lots of oxygen. This is, of course, if the right hydroponic system is used. If required, flowers grown in a hydroponic wall unit (hanging basket) can be transferred into soil conditions when the season is over. Lettuces grown in hydroponic NFT systems can be taken out and placed in a tray or bucket containing a small amount of water where they will keep fresh for some time.

Orchids

Plants such as orchids are ideally suited to hydroponics, because this method of growing provides the necessary control over the roots' environment. Epiphytic orchids grow in a soilless environment in their natural habitat. Terrestrials like a medium with good moisture content and so will do well. An orchid could be grown in pots of Rockwool or Hortifibre (which is very like the orchid's natural root environment), and drip fed from a container suspended higher than the plant itself. Then another plant pot containing another orchid could receive the run-off solution from the one above. Easy automation, a drip feed or a wick system will ensure moisture round the roots. The fertilizer and pH can be easily adjusted to the stages of growth or the type of plant. Rockwool does not decompose, which allows for longer periods between repotting without a loss of structure.

TOMATOES

Tomatoes are best grown using the NFT system. Plants with bare roots (no medium) are preferable, although plants grown in a medium can be bought from a good market garden and transferred to NFT systems. As much dry medium as possible is

Fig 5. Wick-fed plants. This makes a very good window box and, depending upon the depth of the tray, will last a long time without watering.

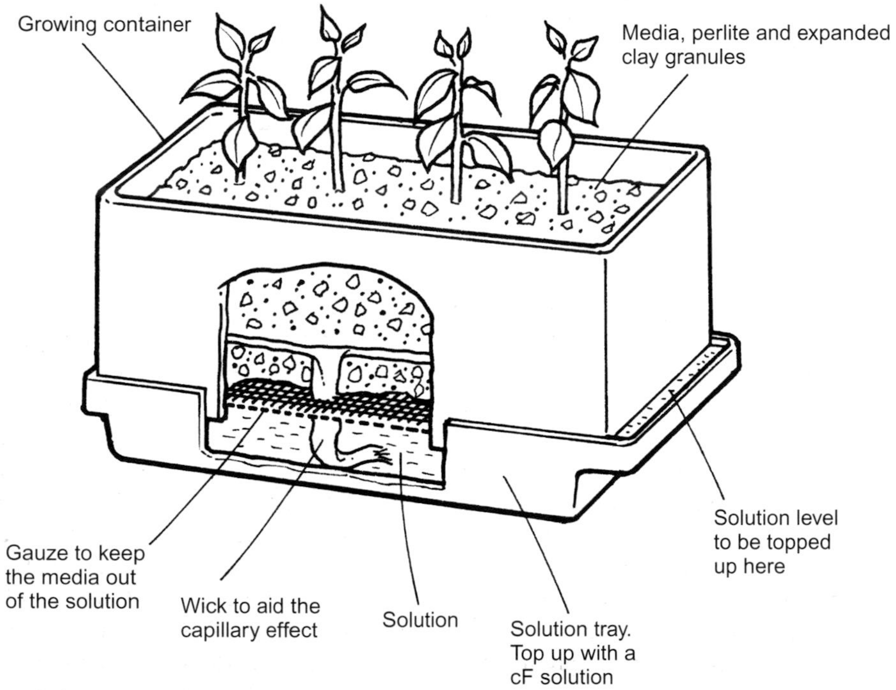

Growing container

Media, perlite and expanded clay granules

Gauze to keep the media out of the solution

Wick to aid the capillary effect

Solution

Solution tray. Top up with a cF solution

Solution level to be topped up here

A METHOD FOR KEEPING TOMATO SEEDS

Cut the tomato into quarters, remove the seeds and place in a jar, add warm water and give a good shaking or even whisking. The seeds can pass through our digestive systems and still grow, so are hardy. Drain out as much water as possible without losing the seed and refill with warm water. Add a dessertspoon of washing soda and give the mixture a good hard whisking. Allow it to stand in the dark for a day or so. Fertile seeds will sink to the base while the residue and infertile seeds will rise to the top. Drain and spread the fertile seeds over a sheet of kitchen or similar thin paper and space the seeds apart. Place the paper and seeds in the sun until really dry. Now either remove the seeds from the paper or store the paper and the seeds in a clean jam-jar with a good lid. Dry some silica gel (obtainable from most chemists) in a hot oven and when it has cooled add this to the jar containing the seeds. This will prevent any moisture causing mould. Keep in a cool place until required.

Plants growing on a tray in small cubes of Rockwool. The base of the tray is kept moist to encourage root growth outside the medium.

removed, then most of the rest is removed by gently moving the root system of the small plant up and down (not sideways) in warm water. To avoid damaging the stem, hold it gently close to the root formation. The plants are then placed in the system with the bare roots spread over a spreader mat on the growing tray.

Growing Plants from Seed

Unusual tomato seeds are available from seed merchants; these can produce plants that are not normally available from market gardens. The seed can be sown and the plants grown in an existing warm area ready for early planting, so saving on heating costs. They can then be trained to produce good root systems over a warm moist surface so that they transfer to an NFT tray easily.

Tomato seeds must have a medium in which to germinate, but some seeds such as edible peas or beans can be placed on the spreader mat from day one. The shell of peas can give problems as it decomposes. When the taproot has developed, the shell will be loose and is easily removed.

A method developed to produce good plants with good root systems involves small cubes of Rockwool

1in × 1in × 1.5in (2.5cm × 2.5cm × 3.8cm) sold by hydroponic suppliers.

The cubes of Rockwool are placed on a tray. The tray is flooded and the cubes soaked for twelve hours in a warm weak hydroponic solution. In the top of each cube of Rockwool a small hole is made, two seeds are placed in each cube and then covered with a little vermiculite. The tray of cubes and seeds is then placed in a warm dark area. The seeds will germinate according to the temperature in which they are placed. They should be checked after three or four days. If germination takes place and they remain in the dark the seedlings will become leggy. If both seeds in the cube germinate the weakest

Seedlings growing on a tray have colour codes.

Training the plant to produce extra roots from the stem.

should be removed. From the first sign of germination the seedlings should be given good light. A thin covering of solution should be on the surface of the tray without flooding it. The plants will put out adventurous roots over the tray when they have filled the Rockwool cube. If tomato plants have been left in darkness for too long and too much growth has been made between leaves, then the plants should be trained to produce roots from the lower portion of the stem.

In this state, the seedlings will be perfect for the NFT tray. The small amount of medium is not a problem and a well-developed root system is a big benefit.

THE GREENHOUSE IN WINTER

If the grower wishes to take hydroponics seriously and grow tomatoes, peppers, cucumbers and melons over winter in the UK, then a lot of thought and attention must be paid to the details of the greenhouse and the conditions that will be presented to the plants.

Amateur gardeners growing tomatoes tend to go through periods of growing in the borders of the greenhouse, on bales of straw and ring culture, until finally the adventurous turn to sharp sand and gravel, from which moment they have reached the basis of greenhouse hydroponics.

Data gained over the past regarding the greenhouse, the position in the garden (sheltered or exposed) and the plants that have been grown in it can be used for the future.

A Solardome greenhouse 10ft (3m) in diameter placed in a position sheltered from the north winds is considered a good choice, but any greenhouse could be adapted using some or all of the ideas given below to grow tomatoes over winter.

A Solardome is a steel and glass constructed dome. However, it has one drawback, which is that the door is shaped to follow the dome. The Solardome looks good and is good except for this small problem, which means that when it rains, the rain falls straight into the greenhouse. Making a porch over the door produces a greenhouse looking somewhat like a glass igloo. However, rain is now kept out of the greenhouse even if the door has been opened automatically due to high temperatures inside.

The dome construction gives this particular greenhouse quite a futuristic look, although it was in fact designed by a German prisoner-of-war who settled in the UK after World War Two. His unique greenhouse design attracts maximum sunlight and is highly effective under northern hemisphere conditions.

The dimensions of the greenhouse are 10ft (3m) in diameter, 7ft (2m) high, and an extra 18in

The Solardome in its initial form.

A fault in the Solardome – the door lets the rain in.

(46cm) can be dug out of the centre. The area without this extra 18in (46cm) is about 82sq ft (7.6sq m). The door is 5ft 6in (1.7m) high and 1ft 11in (58cm) wide and slides to follow the shape. All the glass is sealed, which reduces heat loss due to incoming cold air. Below are instructions on how to build a Solardome. This particular design was to be used to grow tomato plants between the months of November through to October in the UK, so it had to be fitted with designs to cover both summer and winter conditions.

CONSTRUCTING AND USING A SOLARDOME

The following describes the building of a Solardome by the author and its subsequent use over a number of years. The Solardome is situated in the north-east of England, and has therefore been subject to cold northern winters.

After putting down a circular concrete ring base and assembling the frame, the base was dug out in the centre to give the grower working in the greenhouse as much height inside as the ground-water base would allow. Beside the door a plastic insulated water tank was sunk into the ground. This tank was to be the main solution return tank for the hydroponic system. It was anchored firmly into the ground to prevent the ground water forcing the tank up out of the ground in times of high rainfall.

Ventilation

Ventilation is very important. To ensure adequate ventilation, a number of devices were constructed. It was planned to automate the greenhouse and so reduce the time spent in there. All the devices that were utilized and modified are freely available

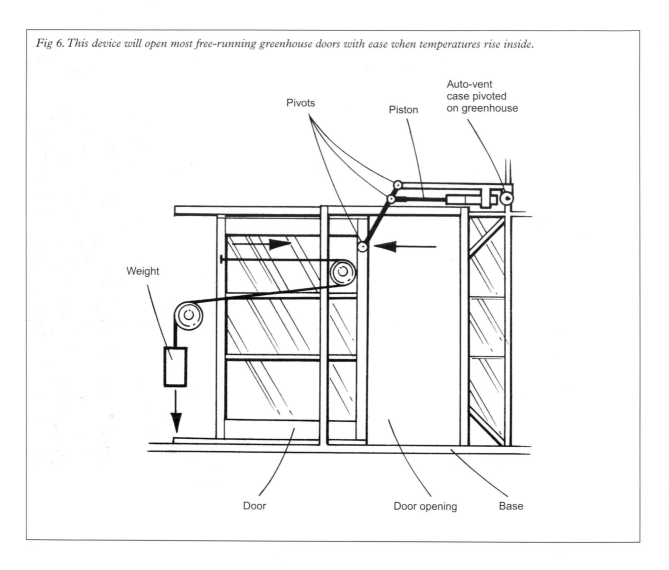

Fig 6. This device will open most free-running greenhouse doors with ease when temperatures rise inside.

commercially. Auto-vents are available from most greenhouse manufacturers and the module used is available from an electronics mail order supplier. This one module was modified very easily to perform all the tasks mentioned below.

Two normal automatic vent units were provided in the top of the greenhouse. The vents are best arranged so that any cold north winds blow across the vents not into them.

A modified auto-vent was arranged so that when the piston was warm, it exerted pressure between the doorframe and the door, pushing the door open against the pressure of a weight.

To close the door, a weight attached to the other side of it by a cord going round rollers pulled the door closed against the cool auto-vent piston. In this way, the door was opened or closed 2in to 3in (5cm to 7.6cm) in response to hot or cold weather. For that bit of extra ventilation, one triangular glass unit was replaced in the lower part of the greenhouse with a plastic pane. A hole was cut in this plastic and a round opening vent fitted in this hole.

The lid of this vent was normally held open by a spring. A cord attached to the lid ran over a roller, into the greenhouse and on to another device,

Opening and closing the greenhouse door automatically.

Close-up of door opening device.

which was made using parts from another auto-vent unit. When the temperature in the greenhouse rose above 72°F (22°C), the expanding piston allowed the spring in the vent lid to open it via levers. When the temperature fell, a coil spring pulled the lid closed against the cool piston. A fan (computer type) with a filter over it can be seen on the photo taken of the vent from inside the greenhouse (*see* Fig 7 and the photos).

However, ventilation did not stop at this point. Fitted in this vent was a fan controlled by a module. The auto-vent piston opened the vent via leverage when the temperature reached 72°F (22°C). A module switched the fan on in the vent when the temperature increased above the maximum setting, in this case 75°F (24°C), or off

when the temperature fell below the maximum setting.

Heating

Heating the air in a greenhouse during a cold winter can be an expensive exercise. However, when the sun does shine, it can get very hot in a geodetic greenhouse, as one or two panes of glass always face the sun, allowing maximum heat and light transfer.

When an electric fan heater is used for heating the air, one module performs two tasks. The minimum setting controls the fan heater and the maximum setting controls the cooling fan (see the detail given in the manual supplied with the module). For switch data and construction details, *see*

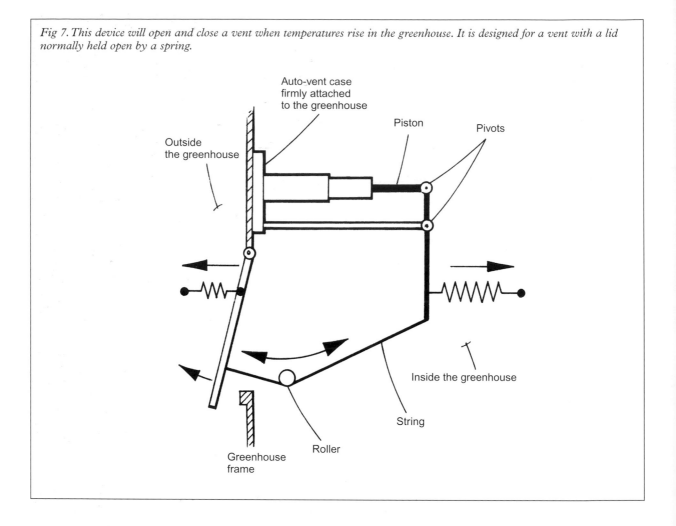

Fig 7. This device will open and close a vent when temperatures rise in the greenhouse. It is designed for a vent with a lid normally held open by a spring.

Auto-vent case
firmly attached
to the greenhouse

Piston

Pivots

Outside
the greenhouse

Inside the greenhouse

String

Roller

Greenhouse
frame

Chapter 8 and Fig 8 and 14. Note that the diodes must be wired the correct way round. For this use the temperature sensor sold with it is fitted in place of the internal pinhead sensor. This external sensor must of course be placed in the greenhouse.

Raising the air temperature far higher than necessary and then allowing it to cool to the required temperature is wasteful. The higher the grower takes the greenhouse temperature above the external temperature the greater the cost. This may be pointing out the obvious, but the high and low swings in temperatures due to bad thermostats a few times per day can make the grower realize just how much extra power is wasted due to poor temperature control. The module used to control the temperature does so to within point one of a degree. The heater used must of course be able to cover the area of the greenhouse.

In the greenhouse itself, all the mains outputs are terminated in a small moisture-proof cupboard on moisture-proof sockets. This gives complete flexibility. The outputs from the control modules (1.5V DC) are converted into 240V AC by relays (*see* Fig 9).

Of course, all mains power comes via a 30mA earth trip unit for safety. Each mains item operating is fused and earthed according to the demand of that item. When it comes to safety the grower should not leave anything to chance. A graphite drawing pencil with the plastic covering removed should earth the solution in the tanks. If a fault did occur, which is very unlikely with modern equipment, the 30mA earth trip unit would be tripped immediately by the current flowing through the graphite pencil to earth.

The Media

It has been found that the best time for planting tomatoes and peppers is around the 1 November in the UK. This planting gives fruit at a time when the cost in the shops is high. In the commercial system the greenhouse is cleaned out in October (depending upon the price of tomatoes) and the seeds planted in November. The plants are placed in position on the Rockwool bolsters in December.

The commercial grower sows the tomato seeds in Rockwool blocks bought as plastic-wrapped 3in (7.6cm) Rockwool cubes. A small indent is made in the top of the cube and the seed placed in this. The seed is then covered with vermiculite and allowed to germinate.

It was decided to follow the commercial system, and as Hortifibre had been offered as a trial and Rockwool bolsters could not be bought, the trial went ahead using the Hortifibre bolsters while planting the seed in Rockwool cubes.

Vent opening and the fan from inside the greenhouse.

Vent opening from outside the greenhouse.

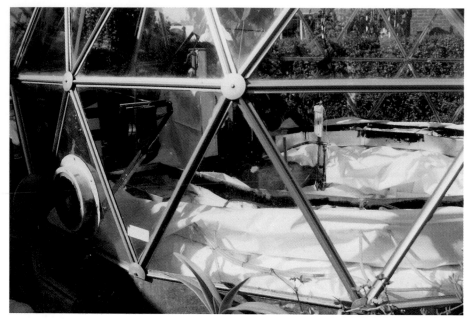

Vent opening and the circular flood and drain unit.

The 3in (7.6cm) cubes of Rockwool were purchased, the seeds planted and covered with vermiculite. The Rockwool cubes and seeds were placed in a tray, soaked in a weak solution for twenty-four hours at around cF5 at 77°F (25°C) then all the excess solution drained off. The seeds were kept moist at around 72°F (22°C). The cube was not allowed to dry out nor was it left flooded. Once a media of this type has dried out it is very difficult to have the whole area moist again. When growth appeared the cubes and seedlings were placed in full light. To extend the daylight hours the seedlings were placed with the growing tip close (not close enough for the seedling to feel the heat) to a 20W low energy fluorescent lamp (100W equivalent) for a few hours. Next morning the plants went back into the daylight again. They must have seven hours of darkness. The plants were kept at 61°F (16°C) overnight and 66°F (19°C) during the day. When the cube was almost dry, it was flooded with a solution of cF5 at pH6 and allowed to drain fully again. This was repeated over and over. Commercial growers follow similar lines, but use very strong lighting during the seedling stage.

When the plants have formed a good root system they are placed on the bolster in contact with the pre-soaked medium in the bolster.

HORTIFIBRE BOLSTERS

Hortifibre gives very good results for short-term crops. Hortifibre is a French idea to replace peat. Peat has been used in large quantities over the years to the detriment of the environment. Hortifibre is composed of compressed lignocellulose fibres with a good air/water equilibrium level. These fibres are then treated and blown into bolsters to give the density that suits the plants being grown. However, it is fully organic and so when it had been used in a flood and drain system for ten months it decomposed and became compact to the point where the air/water ratio was being lost. Even with a good slope it was not draining enough to pull air into the fibres. A mix of perlite with the Hortifibre would have enabled a longer season.

FLOOD AND DRAIN IN THE SOLARDOME

The early system decided upon for this unusually shaped greenhouse was a flood and drain system comprising a circular trough, 15in wide × 3in deep × 22ft total length (38cm × 7.6cm × 6.7m) made out of tin sheet and arranged around the greenhouse, leaving the door free. At one end of the

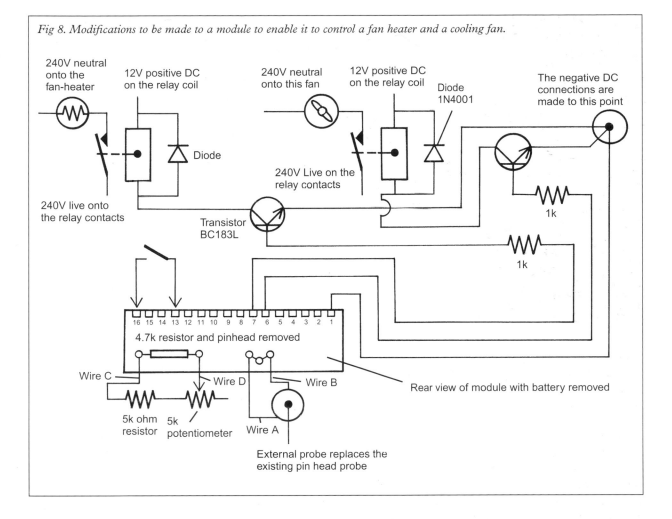

Fig 8. Modifications to be made to a module to enable it to control a fan heater and a cooling fan.

trough a drainage point was made; this was positioned over a 12gal (55l) plastic insulated water tank (main tank) that had been sunk in the ground during the greenhouse construction. The rest of the 22ft (6.7m) trough was arranged around the greenhouse. A good steady slope down to the main tank was provided to ensure good drainage over the full length. This trough was then lined with plastic to prevent the solution coming into contact with the tin sheeting. A similar design could be adapted for one or both sides of an 8ft × 6ft (2.44m × 1.83m) greenhouse, remembering that only plastic should be in contact with solution. A wood construction lined with plastic could be used or a plastic tray.

The solution was then pumped at a high flow rate to each Hortifibre bolster arranged in and around the trough. A timer controlled this pump, which was placed in the main tank sunk into the ground. The timer allowed seven periods of 'on' (flood) per day and, of course, seven off. The on times were adjusted to flood the bolsters, the flow from the pump being greater than the rate of drain from slots cut in the base of the plastic bolsters. The on times were also adjusted to match the size of the plant and the time of the year. In this early system, as the plants took up solution (water and nutrients), the level in the main tank was maintained by topping up with a solution of the same cF as the original solution.

The greenhouse was designed to be able to manage on its own with established tomato plants growing for periods of one to two weeks in midsummer.

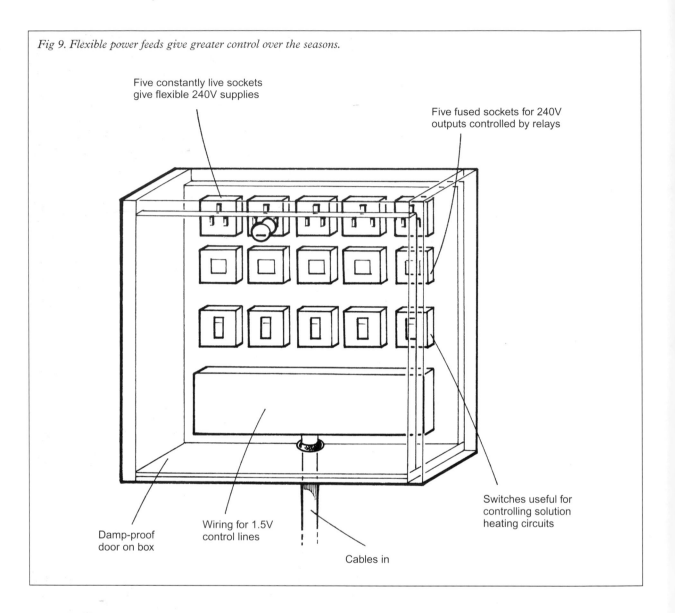

Fig 9. Flexible power feeds give greater control over the seasons.

Five constantly live sockets
give flexible 240V supplies

Five fused sockets for 240V
outputs controlled by relays

Switches useful for
controlling solution
heating circuits

Damp-proof
door on box

Wiring for 1.5V
control lines

Cables in

With this in mind, a 40gal (182l) container was positioned outside the greenhouse; this held solution of the same cF as the main tank. A second pump maintained the level in the main tank by topping it up from the container outside the greenhouse. To control the second pump, a pressure unit from an automatic washer was used. This was fitted and sealed into the top of a length of 1.25in (3.2cm) diameter plastic pipe with a two-tube epoxy resin adhesive making the joint airtight. The bottom of the pipe was left open and fully inserted at an angle

of 90 degrees into the main tank. When the level of the solution in the main tank fell to a set level, pressure in the pipe was reduced. The pressure switch had 1.5V DC connected to one side of its contacts, so that when these contacts closed, as the pressure fell, 1.5V DC positive was put out to the base of a transistor, switching it on. This switched on a relay providing power to the pump (see Fig 10). Solution was then pumped to the main tank until the air inside the pipe was compressed. This switched off the pressure switch, the transistor, the relay and the

Tomato plant in a cube of Rockwool.

Tomato plants developing good root systems in Rockwool cubes.

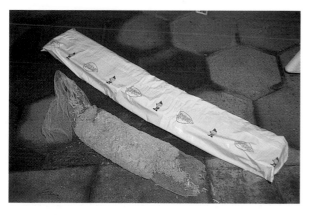

A Hortifibre bolster showing the contents in netting.

A rockwool bolster showing drip-feed lines into the top of the cubes. The clear plastic tube contains carbon dioxide.

Circular flood and drain construction, with feed pipes all around.

Flood and drain unit ready for the bolsters.

The circular flood and drain unit with tomatoes.

pump until the next cycle. A gap must be left between the supply pipe from the container and the main tank. This is to prevent the solution flowing due to a siphoning action after the pump has switched off. In this system, all the solution was changed when the two or three weeks had passed as it was being left for too long between changes and the nutrient balance was being lost. This took place during the summer months so the solution in the container was not heated and the mature tomato plants and the greenhouse managed fine for these short periods of time on their own.

The solution in the 12gal (55l) main tank was heated using a glass 300W fish-tank heater during the winter months. It was found that a small wattage heater could not raise the temperature of the solution to the required degree, so a 300W heater with a thermostat incorporated was used. The larger heater was on for less time and able to cope with the temperature difference.

For safety, avoid contact with the solution while the power is on the heater. To remove a cracked or broken heater, even with a 30mA switch in circuit and the solution earthed, the power must be switched off first. To perform any maintenance on

the heater, *switch off the power to the heater* while it is in the solution and allow half an hour for it to cool before removing it from the solution. If it has just been powered up, it will take some time to cool down and could crack the glass if removed too soon. Lastly, mount the heater away from the sides of the tank if heat is likely to damage the material from which the tank is made.

It was found that the solution in the main tank required extra aeration; bubbles rising would maintain movement in the solution in the tank also. To achieve this, an air pump was fixed to a cane halfway round the 22ft (6.7m) trough. This was a 4W model and it did three jobs. Firstly, the air output was fed to a ceramic air stone in the base of the return 12gal (55l) solution tank, increasing the oxygen content of the solution. Secondly, the solution was kept moving, mixing it continually. Thirdly, the pump was mounted on the cane in such a way that its vibrations could still be felt. Strings attached to the cane holding the air pump went in two directions and were attached to canes at both ends of the trough. The plants were attached loosely to these strings. When the first trusses were in flower the vibration acted as an

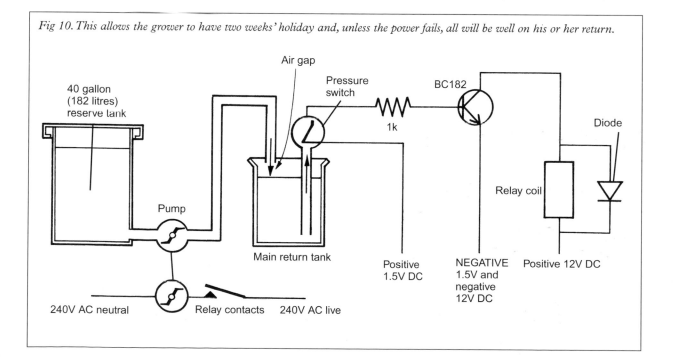

Fig 10. This allows the grower to have two weeks' holiday and, unless the power fails, all will be well on his or her return.

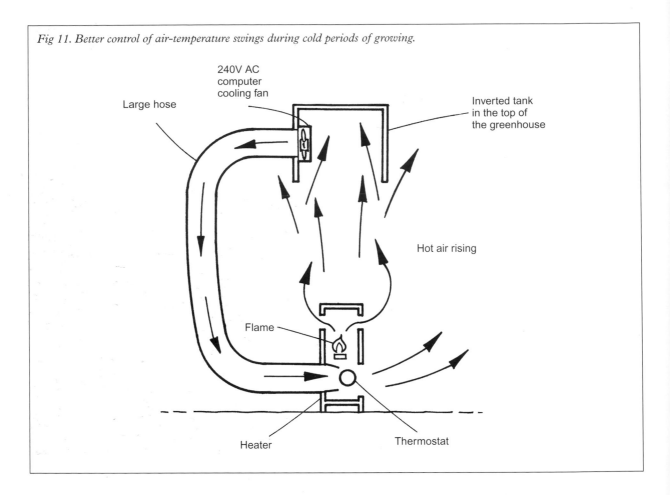

Fig 11. Better control of air-temperature swings during cold periods of growing.

240V AC computer cooling fan

Large hose

Inverted tank in the top of the greenhouse

Hot air rising

Flame

Heater

Thermostat

artificial bee, giving 100 per cent flower set early in the year. Obviously, the canes and air pump have to be firm enough to stop the plants being shaken to bits!

At this point, the module in the garage controlled a 2kW electric fan heater in the greenhouse and a fan for ventilation. Gas heating was considered and tried as an alternative. It was pointed out that this method of heating would have the benefit of increasing the carbon dioxide in the air during daylight hours. This sounded fine and was tried. Heating the air with gas increased the carbon dioxide during the day, but it also increased it at night to a higher degree along with an unacceptable level of toxic gases. With the thermostat on the gas heater in control, the temperature regulation was poor. The flame of the gas fire had ample fresh air fed to

it by air flowing through a small pipe directly from outside to below the flame. Disaster struck in the form of brown edges on the leaves of the plants, rather like that of calcium deficiency. While the problem could have been caused by calcium deficiency, as the hydroponic mixture contained every major and trace element in the correct proportion other causes were looked for first. One other cause could have been poor root systems, but the roots were perfect. It came down to the gas. After the heating was returned to electricity, the problem was cured.

Temperature differences between the top and bottom of the greenhouse were high, so in an effort to reduce this, the following idea was implemented. A round hole was cut in the side of a small plastic container, and a 4in (10cm) computer-cooling fan was fixed in this hole. Then a length of 4in (10cm) flexible ducting was attached to the output of this fan. The fan then sucked the very warm air from inside the plastic container suspended in the top of the greenhouse above the heater and blew it on to the thermostat controlling the heaters and into the lower level of the greenhouse. As a result, the temperature swing beside the plants in the greenhouse was reduced to 1 or 2 degrees either side of that required, even when it was very cold outside.

The high air temperatures in the top of the greenhouse in contact with the extremely cold glass give a high heat loss, so measures were taken to reduce the heat difference between the top and bottom of the greenhouse. Bubble plastic between the glass and the hot, moisture-laden air reduced both the condensation and the heat loss.

During the short periods of winter daylight, an 80W warm fluorescent fitting or a 125W mercury tube was used as supplementary lighting. A time switch controlled the lighting. This was to ensure that the plants not only had the required period of light, but also the required period of darkness. During the 'on' period, which is set on the time switch, a module switches the light on if the daylight falls below a set level. The same type of module is used throughout but with different sensors fitted, in this case a light-dependent resistor. The grower sets a reading on the module at which the intensity of the natural light is adequate, and when the light intensity falls below this level switching takes place. (*See* full details in Chapter 8 and Fig 3). Instead of the platinum probe an LDR was connected. The 1.5V DC from pin 7 on the module switches on the transistor, which switches on the relay. When the contacts of the relay are operated the light is switched on.

A device fitted in dehumidifiers can detect high humidity. This device employs a strip of material that expands when moist. The material is held taut by a spring. When it expands, a micro-switch is operated which switches on power to extra heating. The resulting warmer air can then hold more moisture. This is vapour pressure deficit (VPD). (*See* also Fig 12, for reducing the humidity. Fig 12 does not involve a module.) The 1.5V DC from the humidity switch is placed on the base of the tran-

A side vent, plus a 4in (10cm) white pipe to control the heater thermostat.

sistor switching it on. This in turn switches on the relay, which switches on the extra heating.

Lately, the lighting has been changed to use a number of 20W low-energy flourescent lamps (equivalent to 100W each), which are positioned close to the tops of the plants.

EXPERIMENTING WITH NFT IN THE SOLARDOME

After the successful circular flood and drain unit came a number of NFT systems of one form or another in the 1980s, each an improvement on the previous one. In those early days, information on hydroponics was always very difficult to locate; it

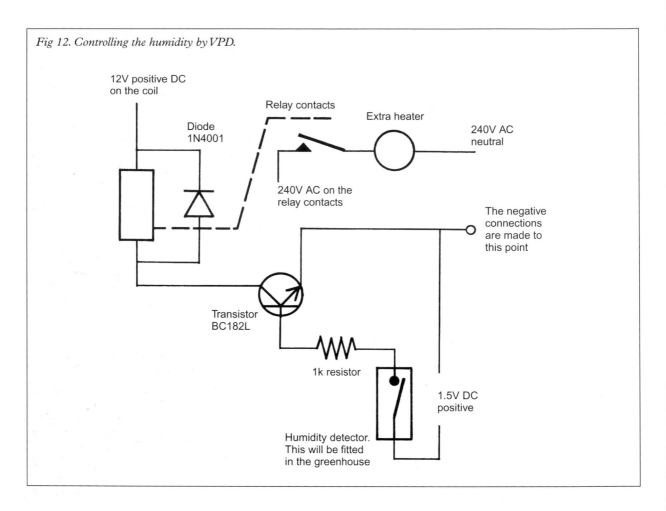

Fig 12. Controlling the humidity by VPD.

was known that commercial growers in Holland were using hydroponic systems along with commercial mixes of nutrients but the amateur was excluded. After numerous telephone calls to far-flung places over the years, a company (Nutriculture Ltd) was located who were able to supply small 4W submersible solution pumps with small quantities of a two-part powder mix of hydroponic chemicals and commercially made Gro-Tanks. Then two other hydroponic suppliers, Growell and Growth Technology, came on the scene. Now information is freely available along with commercial systems and nutrients in two packs and single-liquid mixes.

To prepare for the new NFT systems, the opportunity was taken to make more modifications. The greenhouse base inside was covered with a level layer of sharp, washed river sand. On top of this a sheet of strong plastic (the type used in house construction as a damp course for concrete floors) was laid. Where the tanks were to sit, the strong plastic sheeting was covered with white/black plastic sheeting to exclude light. This was to prevent the damp sand producing moss or algae when exposed to light. The insulation in the centre of the floor was increased to 3in (7.6cm) thick using blocks of a type of hard polystyrene used in house construction. The centre portion was now isolated from the sides and the ground was covered with 1ft sq (0.3m sq) paving stones; these were painted with black flooring paint so that they would absorb heat. This kept the warm air in the greenhouse from the cold ground; any heat provided by the daytime sun was stored by

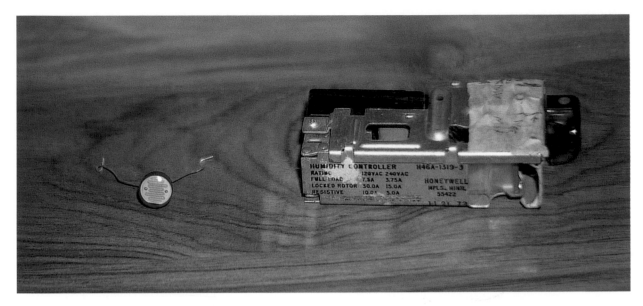

Close up of an LDR and a humidity switch.

The greenhouse at night.

The green top-up tank, thick insulation on the floor and firm supports for the tank.

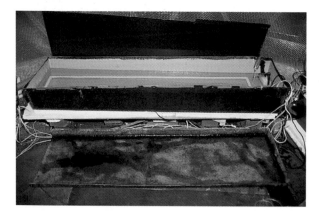

Gro-Tank with the tray on the floor in front.

Low-pressure float valve, pump and glass heater with thermostat.

the black flooring and released at night (a night store heater without running costs).

Homemade NFT systems that had replaced the circular flood and drain unit were themselves replaced with three Gro-Tanks. These were black fibreglass tanks, 90in × 14in (2.28m × 35.5cm), with a flat sloping tray also made from fibreglass (the tray has since been changed to moulded plastic by the manufacturer). This tray covered almost the full length of the fibreglass tank. A gap of about 6in (15.2cm) is left at one end of the tank between the tray and the tank where the 4W water pump is immersed, complete with a filter on its intake. The output of the pump is fed up on to the tray and due to the slope the solution runs down and returns to the tank at the other end.

During very warm sunny days, transpiration (the evaporation of water from the plant leaves) is very high and the plants will take up water and very little of the compounds. In a closed NFT system (recirculated) the water level must be maintained or, as the plants remove water, the concentration of the compounds remaining in the tank will be increased (the cF will rise).

The level of the solution in the three operating Gro-Tanks was maintained by replacing the water used by the plants. To achieve this, a high-pressure float valve was fitted in the green-coloured water tank and fed with water from the mains via a non-return valve. This water tank, positioned with its base around 12in (30.5cm) above the three Gro-Tanks, supplied water to low-pressure float valves fitted in each Gro-Tank; as a result, the solution in all three Gro-Tanks was kept at a constant level.

The cF (solution strength) was constantly monitored and maintained automatically by another module of the same type. All the modules involved in different functions were mounted and connected with other components by wiring between block terminals. This gave maximum flexibility during experiments. Data gained from these modules over the years have led to the much simpler arrangement used now.

Tomatoes, melons, mini cucumbers and peppers can all be grown in the same solution at the same time.

If flowers are chosen, this same solution will also give very good results, although special bloom

A number of modules and relays formed the original control unit.

A crop of melons.

A red, green and black pepper in the guttering system.

Three Gro-Tanks in position.

Healthy leaves are left on the plant head with the stem going round and round.

A commercial system with plants reaching 125ft (38m) long.

A Gro-Tank with a new plastic tray and insulated all round with rock wool.

mixes can be obtained for flowers and for tomato plants when in the flowering stage.

The three Gro-Tanks allowed experiments with feeds to be undertaken in the same environmental conditions.

A large number of tomato plants can be grown in each tank, but each plant must have good air space above it. To achieve this, each plant is layered alternatively to the right and then the left side, then trained round and round. A tomato plant can reach 105ft (32m) or more in a year. All the lower leaves should be removed below the last truss, but at least 5ft (1.5m) of young healthy foliage needs to be maintained on the head of the plant.

The best way to support the plants is to use a string anchored to the top of the greenhouse above the plants. This is wrapped around the head of the plant until it reaches a lower leaf, where it is taken round and under one leaf and back round and up the stem about 6in (15cm). The end of the string is then put through the string coming down the plant in a loop. To layer the plants round the greenhouse as they reach the top, the loop is pulled out, allowing the plant to fall in a controlled way and a loop is made under a leaf higher up the stem. After a while, the plant moves on to the string of the plant next door and so on.

Using this greenhouse with NFT systems, good crops of ripe-on-the-plant tomatoes were achieved in early April of the following year.

It will be found that the plant puts out exploration roots within days of being placed on the tray. Healthy growing plants are extremely adaptable to the strength of the solution as long as it is not too high, although it must be kept constant. The balance of the major elements and all the trace elements must always be maintained. Make any increases to the cF slowly over a day or so.

The air pump was used in the flood and drain and all the NFT systems and good fruit set was achieved.

WINTER NIGHT-TIME HEATING

With the NFT systems in the Gro-Tanks, economy in heating costs could be achieved by heating the solution to 86°F (30°C) using a heater in the tank below the plants. Good growth took place even when the air temperature was allowed to fall to a minimum of 50°F (10°C) at night from January to March, instead of maintaining the normal minimum of 61°F (16°C). On very cold nights the temperature was often down to 41°F (5°C). Heat from the tank rising through the plants no doubt helped.

To maintain the temperatures in the solution, the three large Gro-Tanks were heavily insulated with loft-type rock wool (not the same quality as the Rockwool used as a medium) all round the sides and ends. The base of each tank also had thick polystyrene insulation pads under them. Over the growing tray was a top made of Corribord (from a hydroponic supplier). This had planting holes cut in round the edges. A piece of rock wool insulation material placed in a black polythene bag was laid down the centre between the planting holes to keep the heating costs down. An electric fan heater under the control of a module tried to maintain the minimum air temperature of 50°F (10°C). The minimum temperature was maintained at all times to within 0.1°F unless the temperatures outside were so low that the heater could not cope. Daytime temperatures were left to the heat of the sun through the clean glass of the greenhouse and heat from the solution. Bubble plastic formed an airlock over the door beside the porch (the igloo effect); the cold air was kept out in this way when temperatures fell as low as 25°F (−4°C) and 23°F (−5°C) at night. Despite all this, sufficient air changes took place to maintain the ventilation required by the plants.

During the experiments with the air temperature being heated up to the minimum 50°F (10°C), a novel form of double-glazing was introduced and found to be very successful. Five bubbles were cut out very carefully from a small piece of *large* bubble plastic insulation; only bubbles that were still intact were used. These were placed with the aid of a dab of paste on the inside of each pane of glass on the top of the greenhouse (for a square pane of glass it would be one on each corner and one in the middle). Double-sided adhesive tape was used to attach the clear plastic (the sort that shrinks when hot air from a hairdryer is blown over it) to the frame around the glass. When the adhesive of the tape had set, the clear plastic was shrunk over the top of the five bubbles using heat. This formed a large double-glazed pane of glass and clear plastic. This procedure was performed on each pane of glass on the top of the greenhouse. The sides of the greenhouse next to the plants were left as clean clear glass. The reason for this is that plastic bubble insulation restricts by a very large factor the passage of light just at a time when it is in poor supply and the needs of the plants are high. This method allowed a higher intensity of light on to the plants in the greenhouse and at the same time provided extremely good

insulation against heat losses at the top of the greenhouse.

As a further experiment, one tank (with plants) in the greenhouse had a tent constructed from bubble insulation placed around it. To compensate a little for the light lost by the plastic forming the tent, an 18W energy-efficient lamp supplied artificial light during daylight hours to this tank and plants. All three tanks in the system then had the solution heated to 86°F (30°C). The two tanks without artificial light and without the tent had the advantage of normal winter light on the plants all the time.

During this experiment the outside temperatures went down to 28°F (−2°C) on occasions. Daylight in the north-east of England in midwinter generally falls between 08:00 to 16:00 hours. The air temperature in the tent tended to be around 54°F (12°C), due mainly to the small amount of heat given off by the tank solution and the lamp, combined with the minimum temperature in the rest of the greenhouse. The condition of the plants in the minimum temperature of 50°F (10°C) with natural light were better than those in the tent with the higher temperatures and artificial light. Giving all the plants natural light without bubble insulation, but with the new double-glazing on the extreme top of the greenhouse, is the method now used in this particular Solardome.

The experiment was impressive, with plants growing in a minimum air temperature of 50°F (10°C). Growers normally maintain the minimum temperature at 61°F (16°C) at night. The difference between the two minimum night temperatures is a big saving on the cost of heating over two to three months.

The 300W solution heaters responded to the self-contained thermostat. The solution temperature in the tanks heated by the glass aquarium heaters was helped by natural daylight absorbed by

---

SOLUTION TEMPERATURE

It must be noted that when the solution temperatures are quoted, it is the temperature of the solution in the tank. The solution fed onto the tray with the plant roots on has cooled to around 77°F (25°C) before reaching the plant roots.

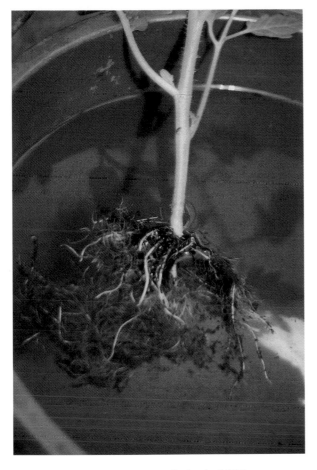

A plant with good bare roots ready for the NFT tray.

Plants in cubes of Rockwool on a moist tray are colour-coded.

Ripe tomatoes on the plants in early April, with daffodils in flower outside the greenhouse.

the black covering. As the plants grew and the season moved on, air temperatures rose and the sun heated the solution.

For winter-grown plants the seeds are germinated around 10 November in the UK. Light was given to the plants from an 18W energy-efficient lamp. It should be placed at least 4in (10cm) above the plant heads as soon as they make an appearance. The lamp should be under the control of a time switch, fourteen hours' on and ten hours' off. If the plants were to share the home heat in the early stages, a south-west-facing or a south-east-facing windowsill would be a good position. Plants can be placed in the system around 15 December, as the root system will have developed by then.

One year, six different types of tomato plants and one pepper were grown. Trouble can be experienced maintaining the labels on plants; the labels are likely to become dislodged or unreadable at some time in the life of the plant. When lots of different plants are in a small greenhouse this can be a problem. To overcome this, give each plant a colour code. Cocktail sticks with a coloured wire tie on each can be permanent unless someone pulls the cocktail stick out.

A colour code can be made up using the base-coloured wire ties, then the same base colours with the addition of white and so on. Putting the plants in the hydroponic system in April or May should be all plain sailing in the UK, as the external environment is improving by then.

A SECOND GREENHOUSE NIGHT STORE HEATER

Commercial growers tackle the problem of humidity by increasing the air temperature, resulting in vapour pressure deficit. Amateur growers can adapt this idea to their own needs. There will be a lot of foliage growing in the greenhouse during the cool times of winter and late autumn and the minimum amount of ventilation is desired to conserve heat. Transpiration from the plant foliage can be high under these conditions; add to this vapour from the warm solution and this could result in humidity problems. During the experiments in the Solardome, it seemed sensible to save the excess solar heat produced by the effective dome shape and to use this to supplement the night temperatures. An attempt was made to keep both these items under control. The following design was incorporated.

The night store heater involved in the original design continued to play its part. This consisted of small concrete paving stones painted black and insulated from the ground.

The efficient design of the Solardome greenhouse results in extreme temperatures being developed during periods of sunshine in the top of the greenhouse. The specification for the new unit, which is currently in use, is to extract as much moisture out of the hot air as possible to reduce the humidity, reduce the extremely high air temperatures during the day and at the same time simulate a night store heater.

Instead of the hot air from this unit being directed on to thermostats as in the original design, it is now blown on to black stones in the insulated water tank to absorb the heat. A metal container, lined around the sides with compressed rock wool (house insulation) has now been fitted inside the old plastic insulated container in the ground. As black absorbs heat, this metal container is filled with a mix of different sizes of black stones (around 1.2in (3cm)) and similar washed river stones (a good depth of stones is an advantage).

To keep an area clear on the base of the container a grid was supported on stones. In this clear area, one end of a long wick that extends into the outer tank was laid. The solar greenhouse is very efficient as a solar collector and as one pane of glass always faces the sun (or where the sun should be) it can result in temperatures around 100°F (38°C) being achieved, too hot for the plants and therefore surplus to the greenhouse at that time of day. Now as hot air can hold more moisture than cool air, when the hot air is blown on to the black stones the heat is absorbed by the black stones and the now-cooled air passes over cooler stones lower down. The air, no longer able to hold such a high degree of moisture, releases it into the base to come into contact with the wick where it is wicked out into the insulated container and drawn out manually.

The air from the fan enters and leaves the metal tank via a large diameter 4.5in (11.4cm) flexible pipe. When temperatures are high in the top of the greenhouse the stones around the point of input and for a good way down will be very hot, but will be gradually cooler away from the input. When the temperatures fall at night the warm air emitted by the hot black stones is blown around the plants, helping to raise the night temperatures.

The fan runs for the twenty-four hours with the air flowing continually in the same direction. If the temperatures remain high over a good part of the day, the heat absorbed by the stones will be blown out at night. On cool but bright days the stones at the top may become quite hot, while further down the container they can remain at the minimum greenhouse temperature. This can result in the warm (not hot) air passing over these cool stones and being cooled before being blown out at night. However, moisture will still be extracted. Under these conditions the overall gain in heat may be small, but it will be a gain.

The average gains in night air temperatures plus the air movement and the reduction in humidity in the greenhouse made the device a success.

AUTOMATING THE GREENHOUSE AND SYSTEM

One of the many advantages of growing by hydroponics is the ease with which the greenhouse can be automated. A 300W glass aquarium heater with a self-contained thermostat automatically regulates

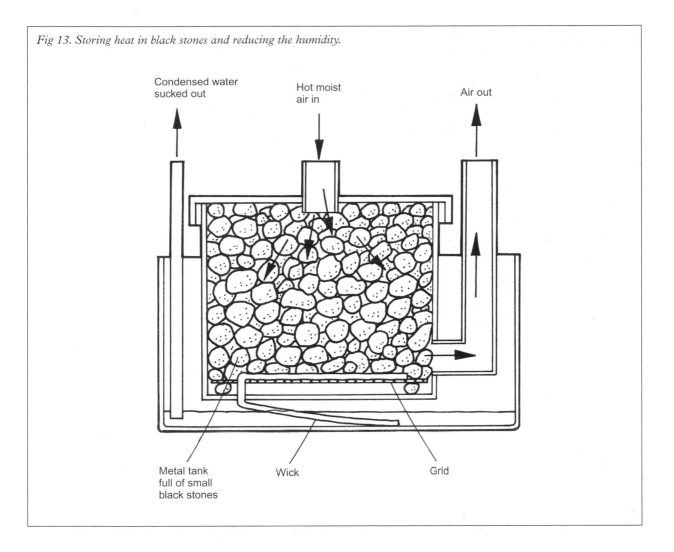

Fig 13. Storing heat in black stones and reducing the humidity.

Condensed water
sucked out

Hot moist
air in

Air out

Metal tank
full of small
black stones

Wick

Grid

the temperature of the solution. A sensitive module can give very good air temperature regulation by controlling an electric fan heater. An electric heater does not produce toxic fumes and gives off a dry heat (gas increases the moisture content of the air unless it is used to heat radiators). A rigid tent, the height and width of the heater, will give it shelter from any moisture that may fall from above. The input, output and sides must be kept open to prevent restriction of airflow to and from the fan heater.

The mainstay of the automation is a commercial module designed to measure temperatures. The resistance of a sensor connected to the module controls the display. Different types of sensors have been chosen to give the results required.

The first of these modules controls the electric fan heater using the minimum setting. At the same time, the same module can give air movement or extra ventilation by controlling a fan during the summer using the maximum setting. This can be achieved using the sensor supplied with the module. The 1.5V DC positive out from the module on pins 6 and 7 switches on the required transistor (*see* Chapter 8 and Fig 14). Depending upon the minimum or maximum setting on the module, the

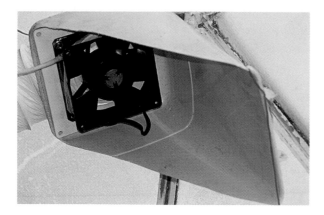

Fan in the roof of the greenhouse draws in hot moist air.

4in (10cm) pipe transports the hot air down.

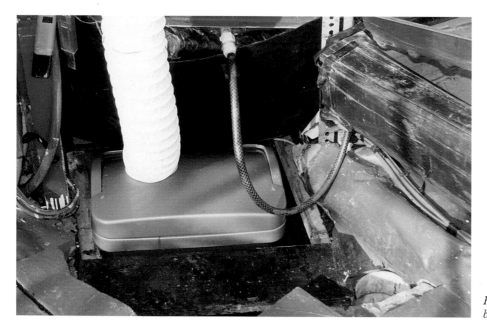

Hot air is blown on to the black stones.

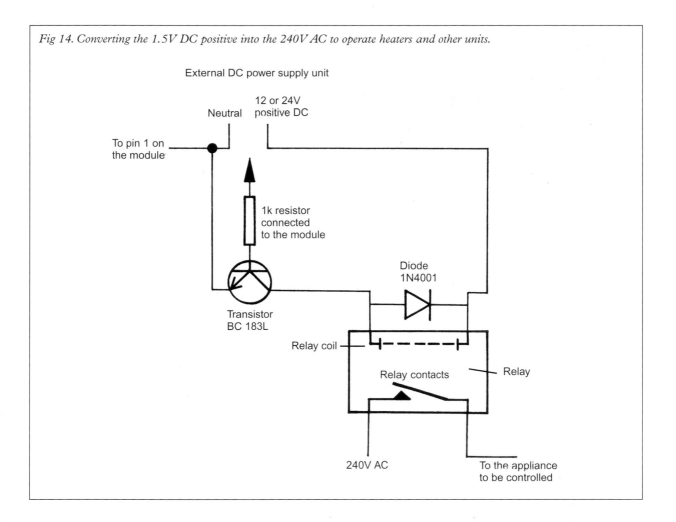

Fig 14. Converting the 1.5V DC positive into the 240V AC to operate heaters and other units.

External DC power supply unit

12 or 24V
Neutral   positive DC

To pin 1 on
the module

1k resistor
connected
to the module

Diode
1N4001

Transistor
BC 183L

Relay coil

Relay contacts

Relay

240V AC

To the appliance
to be controlled

fan heater or the cooling fan relay will be switched on.

Another module controls the lighting with the co-operation of a time switch. This module is modified in the same way as the cF module, but with an LDR (light-dependent resistor) as the probe (sensor) (*see* Chapter 8 and Fig 3).

The time switch decides (with the help of the operator) when the hours of darkness are to be. If the time switch contacts are operated, then the light control module can switch the light on or off.

A unit with a transistor (BC 183L), one resistor (1k) and a miniature relay is required to allow a module to control a mains voltage device. The relays concerned are 1.13in × 1.13in × 0.5in (2.9cm ×

2.9cm × 1.3cm) and designed for direct printed circuit mounting. Each relay can handle a 10A resistive load at 240V AC. This could be a 2kW heater. The coil requires 12V DC. Maplin code for this relay is YX97F. (*See* Fig 14 along with Fig 3 or Fig 8.)

One external power supply (12V or 24V DC depending on the voltage of the relay) can be used by a number of relays if the current rating is high enough; this would be fitted alongside the relays. Both of these items should be fitted in a dry position. These other figures should also be referred to:

• Fig 6 on page 42, as this shows the modifications to the door. The door is mechanically opened when the temperature inside the greenhouse rises above 79°F (26°C).

- Fig 7 on page 44. This shows the arrangement to open a vent mechanically when the temperature rises in the greenhouse.
- Fig 8 on page 47. This shows the diagram to control the electric heater (fan heater) and the ventilation fan in the vent. One module does both of these jobs.
- Fig 11 on page 52. This shows the arrangement to control the gas, electric fire or both economically, which was later modified to control the humidity and act as a night store. Hot air from the top of the greenhouse was pumped down to the bottom, doing away with the temperature extremes. The temperature differences between the inside and outside at the top of the greenhouse give the greatest loss of heat.
- *Refer* to Fig 3 on page 34 and Fig 14 on page 65, as these show the diagrams to enable one module to switch the light on and off. Chapter 8 gives further details of the switches. This module is adjusted to give a figure as a reading (not a display of LLL for 'too low') when it is in the minimum light under which it will be operating. When the light levels fall below the value set by the operator, the light will be switched on. The time switch contacts are in series with the light module relay contacts. In this way, the time switch ensures that the plants have the number of hours of darkness decided by the operator. While the time switch contacts are open the light module has no control. The lights will be off.

A moisture-proof box with a door is provided in the greenhouse. The box is made out of exterior plywood. The door should be inset in the box so that the box itself provides a lip over the door at the top and the sides. A good lead-free paint over the inside and outside of the box and lid helps with the damp-proofing. The box should be positioned with sockets in a location least liable to be subjected to moisture, or special plugs and sockets should be fitted. There should be plenty of room for plugs to be fitted into the sockets when the door of the box is closed (*see* Fig 9).

The cF in the solution can be maintained automatically using the cF meter (a modified module),

---

POWER IN THE GREENHOUSE

- All the power taken to operate the greenhouse must be via a 30mA earth trip switch. This unit should be able to carry all the current. All power units and fittings must have good earth connections. A good earth connection on all metal fixtures in the greenhouse is recommended.
- Constant (live twenty-four-hour) power is required for each of the 4W pumps fitted. Plugs on these outlets should be fitted with a 1A fuse.
- Constant power must be provided for the tank heater or heaters. A fitted thermostat controls each heater. Plugs on these outlets should be fitted with a 3A fuse.
- As well as the above supplies of constant power, a number of switched power supplies are required to allow the module to control the mains devices. Sockets should be fitted in the moisture-proof box for these. The output from the relay controlling the vent fan is fused at 3A.
- The output from the relay controlling a 1kW electric heater should be fused at 5A. If a heater greater than 1kW is required, provision in the fusing, wiring and relay must be made for this. A 1kW heater takes 4.16A while a 2kW heater takes 8.33A and a 2.5kW heater takes 10.42A.

---

using a concentrated hydroponic solution such as Ionic. In this case, for automatic control of the cF only one liquid valve would be required instead of two. Ionic is a single-pack mix of very concentrated elements and as such for manual cF control it is a simple matter to add a single measured amount to each tank after testing with a conductivity meter. In automatic operation, when the strength (cF) of the solution falls below the set point on the module, 1.5V DC positive is put out to the base of the transistor by pin 7, switching on the transistor, the transistor switches on the relay, and the relay contacts close switching on the 12V or 24V to the low-pressure liquid valve or valves (*see* Fig 14).

The cF and pH should be checked at regular periods in the main tanks, although with Ionic the pH tends to stay reasonably steady, due to the manipulation of electrical charges of the various elements in the mix.

The output from the relay controlling the cF via these valves is fed to special sockets. These sockets

Power box in the greenhouse.

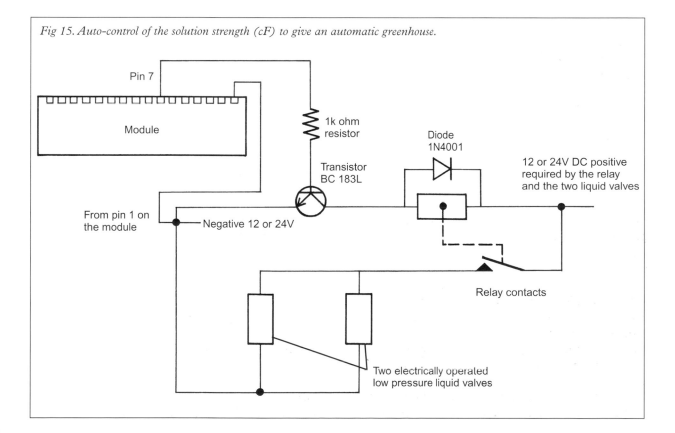

Fig 15. *Auto-control of the solution strength (cF) to give an automatic greenhouse.*

Pin 7

Module

1k ohm resistor

Transistor BC 183L

Diode 1N4001

12 or 24V DC positive required by the relay and the two liquid valves

From pin 1 on the module

Negative 12 or 24V

Relay contacts

Two electrically operated low pressure liquid valves

will have 12V or 24V on them according to the type of valve fitted. Precautions must be taken to prevent a mains-operated item being inserted in these outlets. The fuse on the 12V or 24V power unit could be blown or the unit damaged if care is not taken to prevent this. ***If in any doubt about handling electrical wiring, it should be left to a qualified electrician.***

CHAPTER 6

Hygiene in the Greenhouse

When plants are grown in a confined area such as a greenhouse, the grower needs to give that bit of extra attention to cleanliness and general hygiene. If the time devoted to growing the plants is going to be worthwhile, then sensible precautions should be taken.

- Dead waste should be cleaned up as it occurs. Dead or decaying plant matter is best moved away from inside the greenhouse to the compost unit.
- The grower should organize working on the compost and working in the greenhouse as two separate tasks, preferably on different days.
- Algae or moss found between panes of glass (anywhere in the greenhouse) should be removed by using high-pressure water or scraped off with a thin piece of plastic.
- Algae or moss found growing on the floor in a position receiving strong light should also be removed and the area covered with dense black plastic sheeting.
- Dead flowers on tomato plants drop off as the tomato underneath grows. If this material or any like it falls on a leaf, then where damp conditions exist, such as in a heated greenhouse in winter, fungus problems could result later on.
- New greenhouses should be designed to avoid small pools of stagnant water forming out of sight, as these could be a breeding ground for sciarid fly and other pests.
- The grower should provide the greenhouse with a firm base that can be easily kept clean.
- Tomatoes have a habit of falling off when being picked, so areas should be avoided where they can roll to and be missed, such as under or behind containers. *The rule is, all debris should be removed.*

- The grower should avoid working with soil then going into the greenhouse and working with the hydroponics solution.
- The filters on the pumps should be cleaned at intervals right through the season.

CLEANING OUT AT THE END OF THE SEASON

Growing by hydroponics in a greenhouse requires a few extra precautions. When the growing season is over in a hydroponic greenhouse, the grower should:

- remove the plants
- clean all surfaces with soap and water, removing any dried-on debris
- remove any dust or debris from the tanks
- clean out the tanks properly
- clean the surface of the glass heaters and clean or change the filters on the pumps.

Any items that can be immersed in water should be cleaned in a strong solution of a bleach containing sodium hypochlorite (chlorine). The glass and the structure can also be washed with this. This bleach solution will remove algae and clean the green-house glass at the same time. A strong solution should be flushed through all the pumps and pipework, and the surfaces of the tanks and floor washed with this as well. Safety considerations should be uppermost – rubber gloves should be worn and precautions taken to protect the eyes from splashes. The alternative to bleach could be the solution used to disinfect home-brewing equip-ment or a 2 per cent solution of formalin. The sys-tem should be flushed with clean water when this is complete. It is important that the grower avoids using wire wool anywhere near the pumps, as debris from this will be attracted to the magnetic field of the pump, resulting in pump failure.

Dirt of any sort left in the greenhouse until the next planting can harbour spores, thereby wasting all the time spent cleaning out the previous season.

PEST CONTROL

Biological Control

Food free from pesticides and other toxic substances is well worth that extra effort. Beneficial insects can be placed in with the plants to achieve this. Predatory mites and parasitic wasps feed on other insects and mites, while parasitic insects lay their eggs into the eggs, pupae or larvae of selected host pests. One difficulty is that once a decision has been made to take the path of introducing natural pest control, then only chemicals recommended by the supplier can be used. Substances such as fatty acids can be sprayed to cut the numbers of pests to controllable numbers before the natural control insects are introduced, but even fatty acids (soft soap) will have a bad effect on the natural control insects, as well as on the pest itself. Advice should be sought from the supplier of the friendly insects.

Natural beneficial insects are also susceptible to chemicals. Each pest has its predator; introducing a predator for one pest then finding another pest of a different type, will require the introduction of a different predator for the second pest and so on.

THE USE OF MICRO-ORGANISM PRODUCTS IN THE MEDIUM OR SOLUTION

Humate and micro-organism products sold under the name of Viresco have been available for around six years. In the view of the supplier, fungicides need no longer be used and insecticides can be reduced dramatically. A micro-organism product specially formulated for use in commercial hydroponics is now sold to amateur growers. An item for foliar application contains a microbial product.

In recent years, there has been increasing concern about the use of pesticides, particularly in food crops. Consumers never know what chemicals have been used in the cultivation of the fruit and vegetables that they buy and eat. Partly in response to this concern, chemicals are increasingly being taking out of use because of the harmful effects that they may cause when the treated produce is eaten.

A good medium should be a living medium. It should be the home of numerous micro-organisms and other life forms representing many genera and species. The numbers, kinds and activities of these organisms are influenced by the food available, the pH, moisture, temperature, aeration and other factors. Some micro-organisms, for example yeasts and yeast-like enzymes, live on leaf and fruit surfaces.

To give an indication of the numbers of micro-organisms present in good soils, it is estimated that the weight of live micro-organisms would vary from about 500kg to 2,000kg per hectare!

The table gives an indication of the numbers of organisms present in good fertile soils.

Bacteria	3,000,000 to 500,000,000 in 1g
Actinomycetes	1,000,000 to 20,000,000 in 1g
Fungi	5,000 to 1,000,000 in 1g
Yeasts	1,000 to 100,000 in 1g
Protozoa	1,000 to 500,000 in 1g
Algae	1,000 to 500,000 in 1g
Nematodes	10 to 5,000 in 10g

In addition, there are large numbers of microbial viruses, slime moulds, insects and earthworms.

Introducing a micro-organism, which will assist growth while avoiding those that do not, therefore sounds a good idea. The result should be a properly balanced solution, a stronger and more massive root system, and a healthier, more stress-resistant plant with the correct balance of nutrients.

There are a number of primary products; these contain around fifty different species of micro-organisms. As dry powders, the numbers of micro-organisms vary from about 100,000 to 1,000,000,000 per gram in the mixes. When they are put into water, the numbers then increase dramatically. Thus, when the products are used, the level of microbial activity in the growing medium can be greatly increased and kept at the higher level. The presence of these products can enhance the growth and subsequent yield of all manner of plants.

At the same time, these micro-organisms can suppress others that cause fungal and bacterial diseases. They will not cure a disease once it has happened, but they can prevent it from happening in the first place.

Encarsia formosa. *The female adult parasitic wasp takes over the larva of the whitefly. (Koppert B.V.)*

Some, such as lacewings, will keep down a number of pests, but the adults are keen to fly away. In most cases, once the pest has been removed completely then the predator will itself die out due to lack of food or host eggs. Gall midges have been found to be very effective against green fly.

Spraying with a soft soap pesticide may be necessary if the pest population is extremely well established or has reached epidemic proportions. Integrated control (this is using the correct sprays recommended by the supplier) could succeed in reducing the insect population to a size that the friendly insects would be able to control. With some sprays, a period of around seven days after spraying may allow the introduction of biological control. A set time must be allowed for the spray to degrade before the friendly insects are introduced. Friendly insects and pesticides do not mix; it can take months for some pesticides to degrade. The supplier should be consulted before introducing the friendly insects. Friendly insects are available by mail order. The material is produced fresh each week and arrives through the post in the best condition for success.

If a decision is made to spray rather than introducing biological control then care should be taken when spraying the foliage. Spraying so hard that the pesticide runs down the stem into the solution should be avoided. If the foliage is sprayed just before changing the solution, any excessive contamination of the solution will be removed.

If signs of whitefly are found in the greenhouse, the parasitic wasp, *Encarsia formosa*, the natural enemy of the whitefly, will solve the problem. It is necessary to have whitefly present in the greenhouse before ordering the wasp, since without them the wasp has no breeding ground or food and eventually dies. The wasp for whitefly control comes on a card as a cluster of black pupae. Out of each black pupa a parasitic wasp will emerge (each less than the size of a pinhead).

Biological control can be very good, although to ensure success it must be used as the producer states in the instructions. Any biological product is likely to appear more expensive than a chemical equivalent on initial purchase. However, under the right conditions it is much more competitive than repeated spraying with chemicals and more reassuring when it comes to eating the produce.

The wasp feeds on the young whitefly larvae and lays its eggs in the larvae of the whitefly. If a parasitic wasp takes over a whitefly larva, the larva will slowly turn black. One parasitic wasp can destroy many larvae. From egg to adult takes around

Chrysoperla carnea. *The larva of the lacewing attacks the prey and sucks out their body fluids. (Koppert B.V.)*

twenty-five days at 68°F (20°C). The temperature should be between 64°F and 86°F (18°C and 30°C) for the best results with the wasp. The parasitic wasps themselves are tiny, only 0.02in (0.5mm) and do not bother the grower. Hanging yellow sticky traps around the tops of the plants will point to the first sign of whitefly and will indicate the time to order the wasp. As soon as the wasp is introduced into the system the yellow sticky cards should be removed as the friendly insect and the grower may be caught on them.

If greenfly (aphids) are present, then gall midges should be ordered. A sugary substance under the plant along with the white shells of the aphids will show their presence. The gall midges come in four small tubs; each tub contains forty gall midge pupae, in the form of the final stage cocoons mixed with moist vermiculite. Temperatures should be above 61°F (16°C) at night and regularly 68°F (20°C) and above by day for the midge. The suppliers sometimes recommend damp newspaper with an inverted plant pot over the cocoons as a base if soil is not present. A pile of damp vermiculite in a tray with a plant pot over the top is better, however, as it will stay damp longer than newspapers. The humidity should not be low and light conditions should be good. Each larva will kill

around 100 aphids in its short life by sucking out the body contents. Ants should be controlled, if present, as they tend to farm the aphids for the honeydew and would kill the midge.

A good control for pests like aphids and to a lesser extent many other insects, like whitefly, thrips and moth eggs, is *Chrysoperla carnea* (lacewing). These are dispatched by post direct to the grower as wafers of corrugated cardboard in a box, which can contain 500 to 1,000 larvae (second stage). The pack should be opened in the greenhouse and held above the crop. The muslin covering the corrugated cardboard should be removed slowly and tapped gently over the affected plants. Then leave the empty wafer in the crop so that any remaining larvae can leave when ready to search for food. The adults are around 0.5in (1.3cm), slim, green with wings with fine venation. Lacewing eggs are green and suspended on hairs 0.4in (1cm) long. Larvae are 0.08in to 0.39in (2mm to 1cm), grey-brown with big pronounced jaws. The pupa is in a hairy white round cocoon. Larvae of the lacewing attack prey and suck out their body fluids. The adult lacewings that hatch from the pupae tend to fly away if given the chance. Attaching fleece over openings in the greenhouse can prevent this to a degree.

Product	MAFF	Crops	Active Ingredient
Bavistin DF	M03848	Protected tomato – foliar spray application. Protected tomato grown in inert substrates – drip feed. Protected tomato grown in recirculating hydroponic solution (Nutrient Film Technique). Protected tomato grown in soil/peat bags – drench application	carbendazim
Proplant	M08572	Protected tomato and pepper grown on inert media/substrates or by nutrient film technique. Protected cucumber grown on inert media/substrates	propamocarb hydrochloride
Filex	M07631	Protected tomato and pepper grown on inert media/substrates or by nutrient film technique. Protected cucumber grown on inert media/substrates	propamocarb hydrochloride
Amistar	M10443	Protected tomato and aubergine (grown on inert media/substrates or by nutrient film technique), protected cucumber, courgette and gherkin (grown on inert media/substrates or by nutrient film technique)	Azoxystrobin
Amistar	M08517	Protected tomato and aubergine (grown on inert media/substrates or by nutrient film technique). Protected cucumber, courgette and gherkin (grown on inert media/substrates or by nutrient film technique)	Azoxystrobin

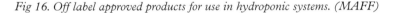

Fig 16. Off label approved products for use in hydroponic systems. (MAFF)

Another major pest is Sciarids (fungal gnats). These are small (0.1in to 0.2in (2.5mm to 5mm)), dark flies with long antennae. During a short life, they can carry root diseases from plant to plant. They favour damp, waterlogged conditions. The fly lays its eggs, which become maggots. These are around 0.2in (5mm) long, thin, whitish or clear in colour with black heads. They live in damp, decaying organic matter in compost. Pools of stagnant water on the floor or under containers should be avoided. The adult fly is just a nuisance in the greenhouse, but the larvae can damage roots if present in large numbers. The fly numbers can be kept down using a small vacuum cleaner, but this is not a permanent solution.

Cleaning out with Chemicals

A letter from the Pesticides Safety Directorate gives this helpful advice to commercial growers, but it is of interest to amateur growers as well:

If chlorine is to be used to kill pathogens or pests when plants are in a hydroponic system then, in the UK this falls within the scope of the Control of Pesticides Regulation 1986. The use of chlorine in hydroponic systems when plants are present to kill pests and diseases also falls within the scope of the Plant Protection Product Regulations 1995. If chorine were to be used to protect plants from pests and diseases in this way then it would need to be registered as a pesticide.

The tables reproduced in Figs 16 and 17 give details for professional users. 'The products shown were taken from the PSD post registration database,

BIOLOGICAL CONTROL

The following biological control measures can be put in place:

- *Encarsia formosa* against whitefly
- *Hypoaspis* mites against sciarid fly
- *Phytoseiulus persimilis* against red spider mite
- lacewings against aphids and other small insect pests
- ladybirds against aphids, although they will eat other insect pests if their preferred food is scarce
- *Aphidius colemani* against aphids
- *Aphidoletes* against aphids.

Product	MAFF	Active	Approval Holder	Marketing Company	Crop	Approval Level
Filex	M07631	propamocarb hydrochloride	Aventis CropScience UK Limited	Aventis CropScience UK Limited	Aubergine (Grown for Cropping in synthetic substance)	Full Approval
					Aubergine (Grown for Propagation in synthetic substance)	Full Approval
					Cucumber (Grown for Cropping in synthetic substance)	Full Approval
					Cucumber (Grown for Propagation in synthetic substance)	Full Approval
					Pepper (Grown for Cropping in synthetic substance)	Full Approval
					Pepper (Grown for Propagation in synthetic substance)	Full Approval
					Tomato (Grown for Cropping in synthetic substance)	Full Approval
					Tomato (Grown for Propagation in synthetic substance)	Full Approval
Previcur N	M08575	propamocarb hydrochloride	Aventis CropScience UK Limited	Aventis CropScience UK Limited	Aubergine (Grown for Cropping in synthetic substance)	Full Approval
					Aubergine (Grown for Propagation in synthetic substance)	Full Approval
					Cucumber (Grown for Cropping in synthetic substance)	Full Approval
					Cucumber (Grown for Propagation in synthetic substance)	Full Approval
					Pepper (Grown for Cropping in synthetic substance)	Full Approval
					Pepper (Grown for Propagation in synthetic substance)	Full Approval
					Tomato (Grown for Cropping in synthetic substance)	Full Approval
					Tomato (Grown for Propagation in synthetic substance)	Full Approval

This is not guaranteed to be a definitive list. It was compiled from the PSD's post-registration database (RAID). It is, to the best of our knowledge, complete as at 24/09/01.

Always read the product label before use to check exact usage directions. © Crown Copyright.

Fig 17. Products approved for crops grown in synthetic substances. (MAFF)

which was last updated on 24 September 2001. Approvals may be subject to change and can be reviewed by PSD at any time and therefore this list is only relevant at the time it was produced.'

The use of chlorine to clean out a hydroponic system when plants are not present does not come under the two regulations above but may come under the Health and Safety Executive (HSE), which is responsible for approval of biocides and non-agricultural pesticides. They can be contacted on 0151 951 3535.

Chlorine is a trace element required by plants in *extremely* small amounts – it can very easily become toxic. Chlorine only kills pathogens it is in contact with; this would be any on the surface of the roots or in the nutrient. Any pathogens that have entered the root cells of the plant would not be affected.

Chlorine is used in drinking water at around 1ppm (parts per million) and can go much higher if the need arises (if disease-causing organisms are thought to be present). It is understood that in swimming baths up to 8ppm are often present. At 8ppm, some plants can be very badly affected while others can accept this level for days. Roots can be damaged.

Using a household bleach to give 10ppm of chlorine takes around 0.0012 pints to 17.6 pints ((0.7ml to 10l) of water. Using the same bleach, the system can be cleaned out with a very strong mix. After flushing with clean water two or three times and a few days of fresh air the system should be fine. Leave plenty of time for the chlorine to disperse.

Formalin at 2 per cent can be used to clean out the system, but the fumes are strong and any plants around must be removed. The big problem is getting rid of the formalin after cleaning out – it is not very nice to work with. For just a precautionary flush out, bleach or the solution used for home-brewing containers would be fine. Rubber gloves should be worn and eyes protected.

CHAPTER 7

Units for the DIY Hydroponic Grower

AQUAPONICS

Aquarium Tanks

Hydroponics can come to the assistance of a heavily populated aquarium by using the water polluted by fish as the nutrient solution. In this way, the nitrogen and fish waste in the water will feed the plants, while at the same time removing the cause of green water (high nitrates) in the aquarium. This is a truly organic hydroponic method of growing plants for the table or flowers for colour.

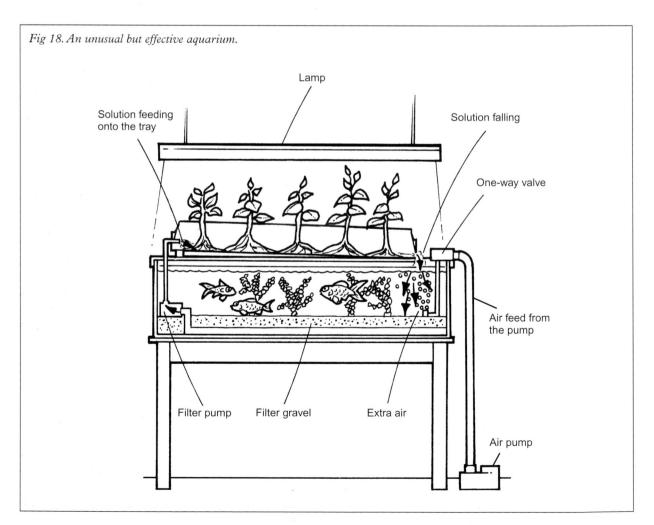

Fig 18. An unusual but effective aquarium.

Lamp

Solution feeding onto the tray

Solution falling

One-way valve

Air feed from the pump

Filter pump   Filter gravel   Extra air

Air pump

Mount the aquarium under a window on a good strong shelf; have the top of the tank just below the window level and fit a tray on top of the tank instead of a lid. This tray will carry the plants and should have a good incline on it (*see* Fig 18).

Water plants in aquariums provide colour and introduce oxygen into the water. However, submerged oxygenators only grow and introduce oxygen into the water when they are in strong light (artificial or natural). Unfortunately, algae grow in strong light also. With the abundance of nutrients present, plants tend to take over the tank and require frequent thinning out.

The tray, positioned on top of the aquarium, can be planted with herbs, salad plants, watercress or flowers; these replace the water plants in the aquarium. Water from the fish tank is forced up on to the surface of the tray by a 4W pump from below a gravel filter on the base of the aquarium. Oxygenated water along with fish faeces and foreign matter is drawn in over the gravel. A helpful breed of bacteria establishes itself in the gravel, changing these items into a nutrient-rich solution that plants can use. Plants with the roots spread over the tray will take out the nitrogen and nutrients produced by the faeces of the fish which have been converted by the bacteria. As the water, now cleaned of nutrients, falls back into the tank it will also be oxygenated by falling through the air. The pump is a small 4W pump and only consumes around thirty-five units of electricity per year. These pumps can be purchased from hydroponic suppliers.

A spreader mat needs to be laid over the length and width of the tray to prevent the water meandering down the centre of the tray. Pet shops that sell tropical fish usually sell under-gravel systems that just feed the water back into the tank. These are easily adapted by extending the output of the pump up to the top of the sloping tray. With a plastic tap in line, the flow can be adjusted to give a film of water (solution) over the spreader mat.

Of course, good light has to be provided on to the plants for a large part of the day to enable them to take up the nutrients. The light on to the fish themselves could be controlled to be on for display purposes only.

Oxygen in the fish water is extremely important. This is why a goldfish in a small glass bowl will stay stunted. Growth of the fish depends on the area of water in contact with the air (oxygenated water), as well as the number and size of fish in the tank along with the amount of food present. The fish can only deal with the food they consume if the water is at the correct temperature and contains sufficient oxygen.

If the fish are tropical, then so much the better; most plants benefit from a warm root temperature of around 77°F (25°C). The solution leaving the fish tank will have cooled a little by the time it flows on to the tray and under the plant roots.

Fishponds

A fishpond with a large fish population has a therapeutic effect and gives an interest to a garden. The sound of moving water along with the movement of fish can help to ease the pressures of the day. However, the pond can become productive as well as giving pleasure. Pond water with a lot of fish in can become unfriendly to the fish, lacking in oxygen and high in nitrates. That same water holds the nutrients required by water lilies, watercress and tomatoes.

The water is sucked up from the pond through a sharp sand-bed filter positioned on the base of the pond. From here, it is passed into the higher end of the second filter, which is fixed in position with a good slope away from the solution input end. It then flows out of the second filter and back into the pond, possibly via a waterfall. During all these operations the pond water is gaining extra contact with fresh air, increasing the oxygen content and at the same time removing any bad air. The second filter can be sited anywhere, alongside the pond, on a wall or in a part of the garden that slopes towards the pond.

The System

The first filter is formed using sharp sand in an open formation wicker container sited on the base of the pond.

An immersible pump pulls the pond water through the sharp sand bed, forming the biological filter (the first filter). From here, it is fed to the higher end of the second filter. After forty-eight

Water is sucked through the sand in the first filter by a pump (bottom right).

hours or so, water with high oxygen content establishes good bacteria in the sand filter (the first filter). The fish faeces, foreign matter and the ammonia from the fish gills drawn into the sand with the pond water are converted into a nutrient-rich solution. Ammonia can also be released into the water by decaying plant material or uneaten food. This is converted as well. When water lilies are planted in the sharp sand of the first filter they consume some of the nutrients produced by the bacteria and give a splash of colour. The fish benefit from

Watercress in the second filter.

a better environment and the water lilies grow and flower without the need for fertilizers, which if used would encourage algae in the pond.

The second filter consists of a rigid tray 6ft long by 8in wide (1.83m long by 20.3cm wide). This tray is fixed with a fall of 10in (25cm) over its length. On the base of this tray a length of spreader mat is laid to prevent the water meandering down the middle. The oxygen content of the pond water is increased as it falls onto the second filter. Watercress cuttings or watercress seed laid on the spreader mat on the tray will take out the nutrient as long as the plants have light (natural or artificial) and heat. This filter must have a good slope and the flow must be reduced to prevent a great depth of water developing. The plants grow and flourish, consuming any nutrients left in the cleaned water. The water is then returned to the pool, completing the cycle.

The pump must run for the full twenty-four hours and can be a small-wattage hydroponic pump. It must be able to raise the water to the required height (from the pond to the tray). An 18W hydroponic pump can raise the water to 4.9ft (1.5m). If the height required is less than this a lower wattage pump will do, possibly a 4W pump. If the flow of aerated water fails for a period of time the bacteria will die and will have to regenerate when the flow resumes.

If watercress is bought from some greengrocers (with a number of leaves on a stem) and then placed in the second filter, it will produce roots from the intersection of the leaves and stem and grow very quickly.

The result of combining hydroponics with a fish-pond will be, given time, a clean pond, no smelly water and algae reduced or eliminated if the plant-to-fish ratio is correct. More fish can be kept in the pond due to the increased oxygenation of the water. The filter does not need, indeed should not, be cleaned out, unless something goes drastically wrong. Nor, of course, do the plants require water-ing. The peppery flavoured leaves of the watercress are rich in vitamins and minerals including vitamin C and iron. Even tomatoes can be grown in this tray, all supplied courtesy of your fish.

Of course, the plants in the filter do not have to be edible, they can be flowers and give a colourful display. This would add a new dimension to the pond and, depending on the plants, would give the much-appreciated colour to the background of the pond.

HYDROPONIC FLOWER UNIT FOR THE WALL

While hanging baskets look most attractive and will brighten up any area, when it comes to the nightly watering the shine can go off. A hydroponic wall unit can be made from square-section house guttering that performs the task of a hanging bas-ket. The initial set-up cost with this DIY system is very low and it is available to be used year after year.

This Nutrient Film Technique hydroponic wall system is very simple both in operation and in con-struction.

Below is a list of the items required for this pro-ject.

- One length of Marley Flowline UPVC square-section guttering 6.5ft (2m) long by 4.5in (11.4cm) wide.
- Four stop-ends for the square-section guttering.

The second filter supports tomatoes on a plant growing in water shared with ten fish.

Flowers growing in the second filter.

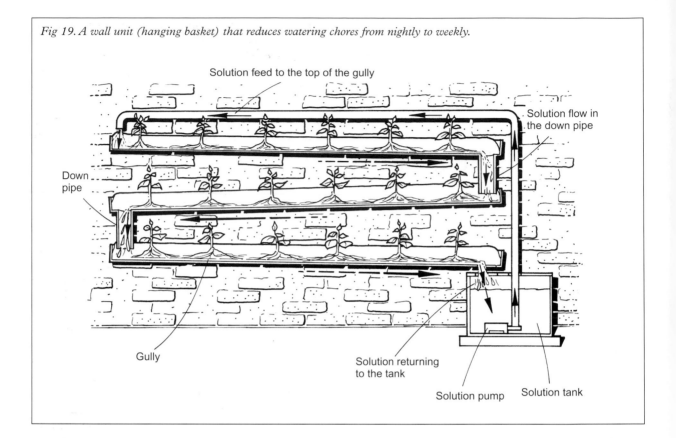

Fig 19. *A wall unit (hanging basket) that reduces watering chores from nightly to weekly.*

Solution feed to the top of the gully

Solution flow in the down pipe

Down pipe

Gully

Solution returning to the tank

Solution pump

Solution tank

Frame of the wall unit.

- Four support brackets for the square-section guttering.
- A length of black UPVC electrical conduit, 0.8in (2cm) outside diameter. This is sold at DIY stores as 'PVC round conduit heavy gauge black 2cm × 2m'.
- Two tank fittings to adapt the conduit tubing into the UPVC house guttering. These are sold as '20mm adapter with male bush black'. An alternative to the conduit and tank fittings could be the downcomer unit sold with the guttering; this is, however, much larger and more suited to the greenhouse system.
- A cold water UPVC tank sold as '4 gallon/18 litres with lid'. If a larger tank can be accommodated then this would give longer periods between solution changes; the nutrient balance should be maintained using a cF meter while topping up with water.
- A spreader mat.
- An 18W submersible pump with a head of 5ft (1.5m).
- A tap to control the flow.

The Marley Flowline guttering is toxin-free. The colour can be white or black. If a plastic is very flexible it is a bad sign. Any guttering made from recycled plastic may contain toxic material; use only UPVC. This item or similar is sold by hydroponic suppliers. If normal house guttering is used, it must be square section not round. Use the brackets sold with the guttering to attach it to the wall.

Making the Unit

Cut the 6.5ft (2m) length of square-section house guttering into two. Fix one end cap on each end of both lengths of guttering. Cut one hole in the base of both lengths of guttering close to the end caps, without interfering with them (these are drain holes). The two tank fittings sold as '20mm adapter with male bush' fit into these two holes, one in each length of guttering.

Fit a length of conduit 0.8in (2cm) in diameter into the male bush portion of each of these adapters. The lengths of these two pieces of conduit tubing will depend on the distance between the two

lengths of guttering and the distance between the lower guttering and the tank.

Fix two of the support brackets for the square-section guttering on the wall, arranging for a minimum of 4in (10cm) fall between one end and the other.

Fit the other two brackets to the wall around 16in (41cm) (or the distance required) below the top brackets, with a minimum of 4in (10cm) fall in the opposite direction. Avoid a vertical fall or the plants will all be on top of each other at the bottom, although the drainage will be very good!

Have the length of 0.8in (2cm) conduit tubing in the lower end of each length of guttering when the two lengths of guttering are in position in the support brackets. This will give a system with the top guttering flowing from, say, right to left and the bottom guttering flowing from left to right and draining into the tank. Now fit the pump in the tank and connect a pipe from the outlet of the pump to the higher end of the top guttering via a tap. Arrange for the 0.8in (2cm) conduit pipe fitted to the lower end of the top guttering to fall into the higher end of the lower guttering. This creates a nutrient flow from one guttering to the next. The 0.8in (2cm) length of conduit fitted into the lower end of the bottom guttering falls into the main tank containing the pump. This completes the closed circulation of the solution.

Preparing the Plants

All that remains now is to put the plants in position and fill the tank with a hydroponic solution. Place a strip of spreader mat over the base of both lengths of guttering, to prevent the solution meandering down the guttering, leaving some roots dry. Make a cover to go over the guttering with holes along its length to accommodate the plants.

Depending upon the type of plant being grown, it may be necessary to provide support. If this is the case, a wire or string tied between the two end caps will enable the plants to be supported using wire ties.

The solution container should be insulated against heat loss through the ground. A south-facing wall would be ideal unless the solution temperature becomes too warm (above 82°F (28°C)).

Solution flowing into the first guttering.

Newly planted flowers in the wall unit.

Wall unit established with flowers.

WALL UNIT FOR THE GREENHOUSE

(Refer to Fig 19 on page 80.) A small system can be made up and fitted on one wall at the side of the greenhouse or a system can be fitted on both side walls or almost anywhere with good light and shelter. A system like this fitted on the north-facing wall of the greenhouse increases the growing area considerably. The guttering sold to go around bay windows enables units to be placed around bay-type areas.

Arrange the guttering on the wall in the formation of a 'V' on its side and use the downcomer unit sold with the guttering to feed into the higher end of the section of guttering below. Pump the solution to the top of the 'V' and place the main tank containing the pump under the outlet of the lower end of the 'V' formation so that the solution runs back into it.

If the 'V' formation is used on both long walls of a greenhouse then one solution tank positioned on the end wall could be used for both systems. In this case, only one pump would be required. In all cases where a submersible pump is used, be sure that the pump has a head that will be sufficient to carry the solution up to the point required in the quantity required (0.9 pints (0.5l) a minute) for each system, twice that for large plants.

A system like this is ideal for lettuce or pepper plants, although it is also possible to grow tomatoes in it. Ample room must be allowed for the foliage.

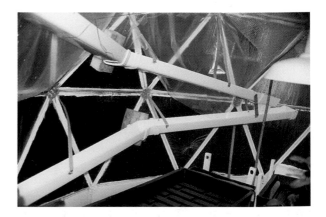

The wall unit idea transposed into the greenhouse.

Showing the wall unit from the outside looking in.

Melons in the greenhouse wall unit.

A UNIT FOR THE GREENHOUSE, CONSERVATORY OR A CONCRETE AREA

This system is very adaptable. A greenhouse, conservatory, porch or even a concrete surface could have a good NFT system as long as a little warmth and good light are provided (natural or artificial light). A bench-mounted system would avoid the need for bending down for those who experience this difficulty. Commercial units on these lines and also a system from New Zealand can be purchased from hydroponic suppliers.

If small plants like flowers or lettuce are to be grown, then a number of gully lengths mounted side by side with dimensions around 4in wide by 2in deep (10cm by 5cm) by the length of the area to be filled will be required. Avoid very long lengths. The Marley Flowline UPVC square-section guttering can be used in this unit. Peppers, tomatoes, lettuce, peas and many other plants can be grown in this system. Support from above will need to be arranged for some plants.

For the bench-mounted system, arrange for a bench sloping 10in (25cm) over 9ft (2.7m). A grower confined to a wheelchair or with back problems could use a bench with a good working height. The lower end of the gullies will overhang the bench and feed into (or be channelled into) the main tank containing the pump, which can be positioned under the bench. This makes a good NFT system.

Peas, peppers and lettuces in the greenhouse wall unit.

Peas growing in the greenhouse guttering.

Red, green and black peppers in the wall unit.

Strawberries and lettuces in the wall unit.

Radish in the guttering in the greenhouse.

Strawberries in the greenhouse guttering unit.

Solution from the tank is pumped up to the top of all the gullies, where it runs back down in parallel and back to the tank again. To give a good flow of solution to each gully a good diameter pipe should be used from the pump to the junction with the gullies. The bare roots of the plants are placed through holes in the covers of the channels on to the spreader mat that has been laid over the full length of all the gullies. For further details, *see* Fig 4.

AN 'A' FRAME UNIT

An 'A' frame unit can be made in order to increase the production of a growing area. Strawberries, lettuce and the like can be grown in these units.

Made on the same lines as the wall unit (*see* Fig 19), guttering is positioned on both sides of the 'A' frame. The number of lengths of guttering going from left and right across both sides of the frame will depend upon the height of the frame, the area to be covered, local conditions and the requirements of

The flow from the top to the lower guttering (greenhouse unit).

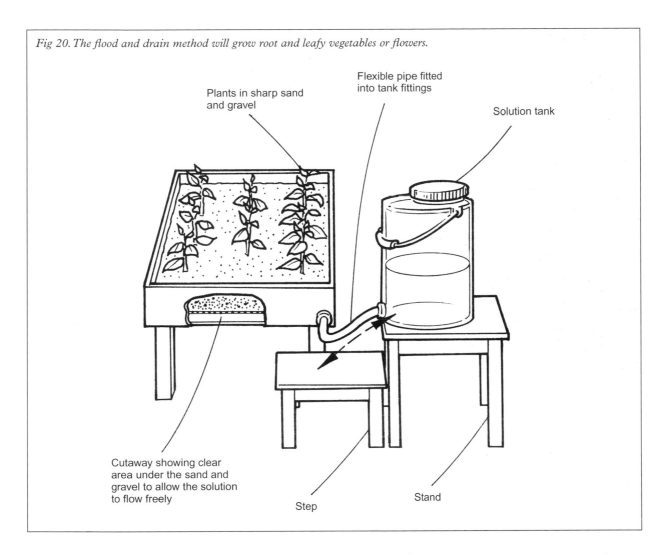

Fig 20. The flood and drain method will grow root and leafy vegetables or flowers.

Plants in sharp sand
and gravel

Flexible pipe fitted
into tank fittings

Solution tank

Cutaway showing clear
area under the sand and
gravel to allow the solution
to flow freely

Step

Stand

the grower. The solution is pumped up to the top length of the guttering on both sides of the 'A' frame, where it runs back and forth and returns from both sides of the 'A' frame to the tank containing the pump. The increase in production from that area of ground (concrete or soil) will be very high.

FLOOD AND DRAIN UNITS

Hydroponics provides a number of flexible growing systems. A well-tried hydroponic unit is the flood and drain system. The plant, placed in a mixture of sharp sand, perlite and baked clay balls is flooded

with a mix of hydroponic solution at the correct pH and solution strength for its type.

After giving the medium a good soaking, all the remaining solution is allowed to drain fully back into a container where it will be available for the next period of flood. As the solution floods in, unwanted gases around the roots are forced out, then as the solution drains out, air with the required oxygen is pulled in, leaving good air-to-nutrient and -water ratios. This cycle leaves the roots of the plant fully supplied with every major and trace element it requires, along with a good ratio of air (containing the required oxygen) to solution of around 40:60 depending upon the medium.

This is a well-tried system that can be set up to require no power; although with a time switch and pump, it can be automated. Over the years, the author's system has grown everything from tomatoes to onions, cabbages to potatoes, all experimental and all a big success. Potatoes do well, but the system has to be emptied to harvest them, and then restarted.

As can be seen from the photos, the system involves lifting the container to flood it and placing it on a point lower than the growing container to drain fully. The original system containing an asparagus and a fig tree split the plastic container after a number of years of strong growth. The fig tree was transferred into a household dustbin during its dormant period. In the spring, the tree looked as fit as ever and continued to produce good crops of figs in late September/October. The tree only needed flooding occasionally during winter; normally there was enough rain to keep it moist.

Building a Flood and Drain System

Two plastic containers are required. One container holds the solution; this should be a reasonable weight to pick up when full and have a handle. A 3gal (13.6l) black bucket with a lid would be a good choice. If the system is automated, then the weight will not be important. The second container will be the growing container with the size adjusted to the needs of the plant type. If it is to be used to grow asparagus, a very deep container of 18in (46cm) or more is required to give good-sized asparagus spears. The roots of the fig tree also require a good depth. Of course, both of these are long-term crops.

On the base of the growing container, place a layer of large pumice, large gravel or brick rubble (no lime or cement if old bricks are used). The rubble should be around 1in (2.5cm) across or large enough to prevent it entering the tank fitting and pipe. This is to allow free movement of the solution, from and to, a tank fitting in the base. On top of this rubble place a piece of 0.25in (6.4mm) plastic or similar non-rotting material (not metal), just smaller than the base of the container. This is to keep the rubble open and allow the solution to flow freely. The container is now filled with washed coarse river sand, fine gravel and baked clay balls. The clay balls are mixed with the river sand to improve the solution retention of the medium. All perlite can be used, but it can be expensive if a large amount is involved and during the flood cycle it tends to float. If all perlite is used, cover with a good layer of gravel to hold it down.

Flexible pipe (as used to connect automatic washing machines or any similar hosepipe) is fixed to the base of the growing container by a plastic tank fitting. Run this flexible pipe to the solution container, then attach it to the base using another plastic tank fitting.

Planting

In the original experiment, two separate systems were involved, one containing a fig tree and the other asparagus. Both plants require a good-sized container. A good fig tree for this system is the variety 'Brown Turkey'. If the tree is allowed to go into winter with large pea-size figs on, they will have a good chance of getting through periods of frost and developing during the following year. Anything bigger is best removed.

The asparagus crowns can be bought from most garden centres and planted in the medium. Allow one or two years for the plants to establish before harvesting, and at the end of each cutting season give the plants time to build up again for the next year. Potatoes can be planted in a system with a good depth such as a dustbin, and if given light and sheltered from frost in a warm area can provide early new potatoes.

As spring approaches, the solution container needs to be raised above the growing container, forcing the solution to flow into the growing container. The height and contents of this solution container should be such that when the flow between the containers has finished, the planted medium just below the surface should be flooded. The two containers are left in this condition for a minute or so to soak the medium thoroughly, then the solution tank is returned to a point on the ground well below the base of the planted container so that all the excess solution drains out. The frequency with which this needs to be carried out will depend on the size of the plants and the air temperature.

A fig tree in a flood and drain unit with the solution container in the flood position.

Flood and drain unit, drain position.

Flood and drain unit, flood position.

First year asparagus, with black plastic over the solution container.

Fig tree in a flood and drain dustbin.

Ripe fig in the flood and drain unit.

Do not allow light to fall on the solution in the container. Black polythene makes a good cover. This is to prevent algae forming in strong light conditions

While the fig tree is producing good crops of figs it is fed at cF16 (less nitrogen) with the pH at 6. When the asparagus is established it will require the same feed. A lower strength (around cF6) will be required for new plants or lettuce if the system is used for this.

This container and system is fine for any plant, roses, tomatoes and nearly all flowers.

Growing African Violets in Flood and Drain

In this experiment, a decorative fruit bowl without drainage holes had a 1in (2.5cm) layer of medium placed on the base. Two African violet plants were purchased from the local garden centre and some of the medium removed from the roots. The roots of these plants were placed with the lower tip of the roots just on top of the 1.75in (4.4cm) layer of medium on the base of the container, and the rest of the medium of vermiculite and baked clay balls was used to fill the bowl up to the crown of the plants, covering all the roots. The crown of the plant should be just below the level of the medium and the lower tip of the roots just on the top of the base layer.

When the plants were established, a leaf was removed from a plant and pushed in alongside the originals. These have produced extra plants. On occasions, the decorative bowl is flooded with water

African violets in a flood and drain decorative pot.

A flower arrangement grown in flood and drain.

African violets in a flood and drain decorative pot.

(keeping it off the leaves), then drained off by tipping it over. The plants have been in this system for a lot of years and now when the bowl is tipped to drain, none of the medium comes out, as the root mat is so large. The plants in the bowl give a good show of flowers at intervals throughout the year; when the plants are in flower they are given a feed of around cF6.

Growing an Orange Tree in Flood and Drain

Drill a row of 0.25in (6.4mm) drainage holes at around 1.5in (3.8cm) intervals around the side of a 10in (25cm) plastic plant pot, up to a height of approximately 0.5in (1.3cm) from the base. Place a mix of fifty/fifty perlite and baked clay balls in the plant pot and arrange for it to reach a height of approximately 0.75in (1.9cm) above the top of the drainage holes. A small plant from a nursery can be prepared by removing some of the loose medium from the roots while it is damp.

Spread the roots of the tree over this medium and top it up with a mix of vermiculite and baked clay balls. Have the roots of the tree sloping down towards the 1.25in (3.2cm) (that is, 0.75in + 0.5in (1.9cm + 1.3cm)) of medium on the base. The base of the trunk should be just below the surface of the medium. Avoid air pockets around the roots by running a cF6 solution in from the top of the pot, draining and running it in again a few times. This procedure should result in the tips of the longest roots of the tree being around 0.75in (1.9cm) above the drainage holes on the base of the plant pot, with the rest of the roots hanging down from the crown. The 10in (25cm) plastic pot is then stood in a wider decorative bowl without drainage holes. Watering is performed using a cF6 solution. This solution is poured on to the top of the planted medium and allowed to filter into the decorated bowl without drainage holes. This takes place until

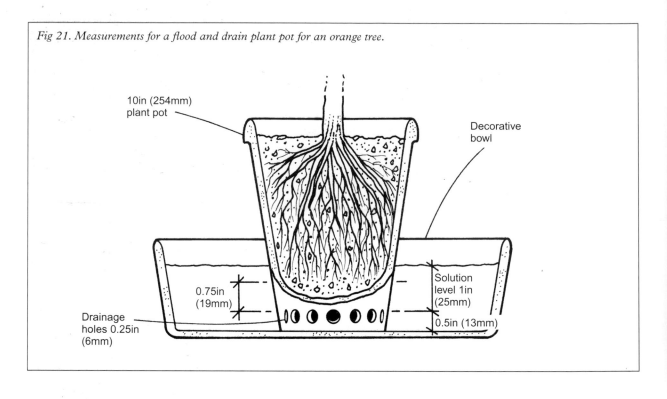

Fig 21. Measurements for a flood and drain plant pot for an orange tree.

10in (254mm)
plant pot

Decorative
bowl

0.75in
(19mm)

Solution
level 1in
(25mm)

Drainage
holes 0.25in
(6mm)

0.5in (13mm)

the solution in this bowl is 1in (2.5cm) above the drainage holes that have been drilled into the sides of the plant pot. Allow the level to fall below this point as the tree takes up water and nutrients, then maintain the level by adding more solution at the same cF to the top of the plant pot, letting it drain to raise the level of the solution in the decorative bowl. Around once a year (sooner if the plant looks unhappy) flush with a low cF solution then replace with a solution of the correct cF. A wider bowl with the solution at the same depth will permit the plant to be left for longer periods without attention.

Artichokes in Flood and Drain

In this experiment, the artichokes were planted in a growing container (in this case, a child's toy box) in a mix of 75 per cent sharp sand and 25 per cent perlite; the growing container was then placed on a stand above the ground. The solution was placed in a bucket positioned under the growing container. A length of hosepipe connected the growing container and the bucket. To feed the plants, the bucket filled with solution was tipped into the growing

container and then replaced under it. The pH and the cF were adjusted to the plant type.

AN NFT AND SAND SYSTEM

This involves a tray made out of either plastic or fibreglass and positioned on a sloping table. The drain-off from the tray is fed into a second container filled with a medium created from a mix of rough sand, perlite and baked clay balls.

If instead of the tray two or more lengths of square-section house guttering are placed side by side and fed in parallel with the solution, a wider distribution of solution would be fed into the second container. This container, taking the drain-off from the tray/guttering, has itself got a drain-off point and the solution from this is passed through a filter back into the main tank containing the pump. The pump then returns the solution to the tray/gutter. This completes the cycle, which takes place for the full twenty-four hours. The tray/guttering has spreader mat placed along the lengths to prevent the solution meandering down and missing

An orange tree in a flood and drain green bowl.

An orange tree out of the drain bowl showing the holes around the base of pot.

some of the plant roots. This unit provides all growers, including those with back problems, the opportunity to grow a mixture of root vegetables along with plants like tomatoes and lettuce.

A HYDROPONIC STRAWBERRY OR FLOWER TREE

Growing strawberries by the method described here is very easy. It leads to savings in both time and effort, not to mention sparing the back. Flowers can also be grown very successfully by this method.

This unit does away with nightly watering, but does require an electrical power outlet. The system described here is ideal for growing small plants (flowers or strawberries) in the house, in the conservatory, on the patio or on a roof garden.

If the hydroponic tree is planted with the right type of strawberry plants, then strawberries can be produced continuously outside from July to the first frost and in the greenhouse almost right round the year.

Alternatively, a good mix of flowers can give that very welcome splash of colour with the minimum of effort. Planted with a collection of 4in to 6in (10cm to 15.2cm) high flowers the tree gives a really colourful display to brighten up any area where natural or artificial light is available.

The construction is very simple using items purchased from a DIY building store and hydroponic suppliers. The tree is made entirely from plastic, as metal must not be in contact with the solution. In the flower tree, a small wattage 240V immersible pump runs in a hydroponic nutrient solution. The solution level must be maintained. Light from a 20W high efficiency fluorescent lamp, provided from 8:00 to 18:00 on long dark days in winter

Artichokes grown in flood and drain.

would be an asset. Following are the items required to make the tree.

- One 'Marley soil pipe with a seal socket' at one end, 4.25in (10.8cm) in diameter and cut to 2ft 4in (71cm) in length.
- A 4gal (18.2l) cold water UPVC expansion tank with a lid. This tank can be obtained from a hydroponic supplier by mail order or from a DIY plumbing supplier. A tank with a bigger base area will give longer times between top-ups but will change the dimensions given here.
- About 9in (23cm) of 2.75in (7cm) diameter plastic pipe.
- Seven plastic nuts and bolts from a hydroponic supplier.
- A round piece of plastic to rest on the plastic bolts in the Marley soil pipe to form a filter. The bottom of a round plastic jug with lots of 0.125in (3.2mm) holes drilled in played this part. This is to hold the medium up above the pump.
- A small immersible pump. It must have a head of 2.3ft (0.7m) (very important). This stands out of sight in the solution on the base of the tank with

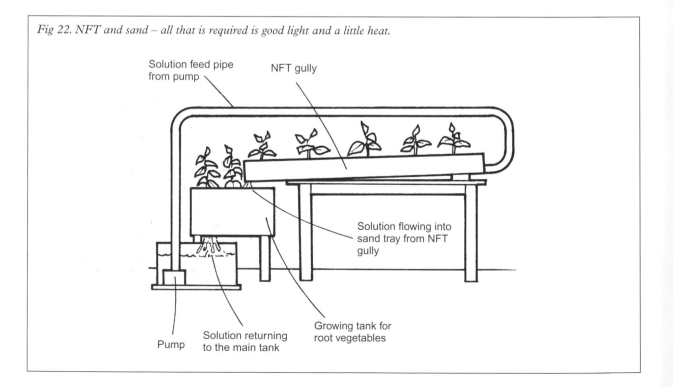

Fig 22. NFT and sand – all that is required is good light and a little heat.

Solution feed pipe from pump

NFT gully

Solution flowing into sand tray from NFT gully

Growing tank for root vegetables

Pump

Solution returning to the main tank

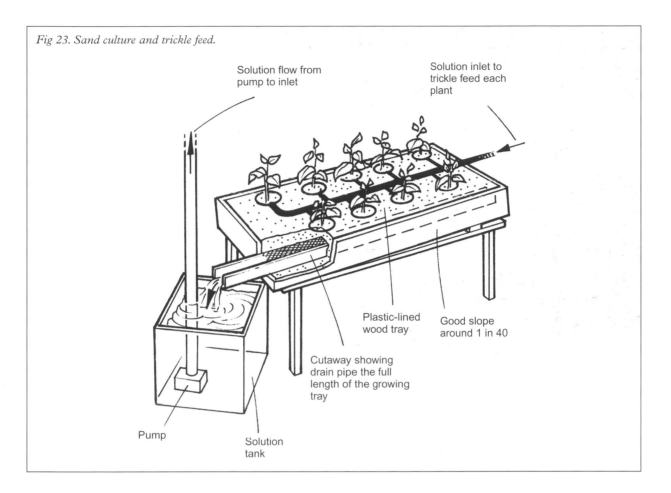

Fig 23. Sand culture and trickle feed.

Solution flow from pump to inlet

Solution inlet to trickle feed each plant

Plastic-lined wood tray

Good slope around 1 in 40

Cutaway showing drain pipe the full length of the growing tray

Pump

Solution tank

an outlet on the top and a filter on the bottom. There must not be any metal parts. The pump used in the tree in the photographs was a 'Macro-Jet MC450 6W at 220–240V with a flow of 430 litre/hour'.

- A length of plastic tubing with the diameter to fit the outlet of the pump, 27.25in (69cm) long. This will connect the pump to the outlet (fountainhead) on top of the media. The fountainhead distributes the solution evenly. If a fountainhead is fitted, this should be included in the 27.25in (69cm).

- A bag of perlite and one of baked clay balls. This is to provide a mix of one part perlite to three parts baked clay balls.

- A length of plastic pipe 2ft 4in (71cm) with an outside diameter of 1.6in (4cm) to make the lips for the plants to rest on.

Strawberry tree planted.

Strawberry tree, showing a good crop.

Strawberry tree planted with flowers.

Once constructed, the flower or strawberry tree can be used year after year.

Construction Details

Please see the photos and drawings for assistance in building the strawberry tree. The tools required are a round file, a drill, a hacksaw and a strong pair of scissors or tin snips. Plastic is an extremely easy material to work with. The whole construction should only take around half a day. Before commencing work on building the tree, reduce the height of the 4gal (18.2l) water tank to give a total height of 8in (20.3cm) by cutting the top off with a hacksaw.

1. The soil pipe (sold as a 'Marley soil pipe with seal socket') has a flange on the base containing a rubber gasket. Remove the rubber gasket and file a 2in wide by 0.5in deep (5cm by 1.3cm) slot in the base of the flange. This will allow the solution in the tank to flow under the base of the soil pipe, while the flange of the pipe is sitting flat on the base of the water tank.
2. On one side of the pipe, drill four 1.25in (3.2cm) holes 6in (15.2cm) apart in a line from top to bottom in the 2ft 4in (71cm) high pipe. Start from a point just above the top of the cut-down tank. This is to take the plants. Now drill four holes on the opposite side of the pipe in line with the first four holes. Stagger three holes in a line top to bottom on both sides of the first line of four holes. This gives fourteen planting holes in total.
3. Make a plastic filter by drilling as many

Strawberry tree construction.

0.125in (3.2mm) holes as possible in a round piece of plastic. The base of a plastic jug could do this job. This filter should be a reasonably good fit in the soil pipe to sit on the ends of the four plastic bolts now protruding into the 2ft 4in (71cm) high pipe. The filter is to prevent the medium in the soil pipe coming in contact with the pump and it must allow *all* the solution to return freely to the tank.

4. Now cut the 9in (23cm) length of 2.75in (7cm) diameter pipe into three lengths 3in (7.6cm) long and attach each of these lengths to the 2ft 4in (71cm) soil pipe on three sides. The same three 3in (7.6cm) lengths of pipe will be attached to three sides of the tank later. This is to secure the soil pipe vertically in the tank. Plastic nuts and bolts are used for this operation. The bolts are fitted inside the 3in (7.6cm) long lengths of pipe so that the bolts extend through the soil pipe. Secure these with a nut by putting one hand up inside the soil pipe. Place a fourth plastic bolt level with the other three in the soil pipe. The sole function of this nut and bolt is to add support to the filter given by the other three bolts. The filter will be fitted later.

5. The pump with a length of pipe and a fountainhead attached will be positioned out of sight inside the flange of the 2ft 4in (71cm) soil pipe. The pipe from the pump that terminates on a fountainhead will pass through the middle of the plastic filter, which will rest on the four protruding plastic bolts. The fountainhead is to spread the solution over the growing medium.

6. The total length of the hose from the pump, including the fountainhead, should be 27.25in (69cm). This is quite important, as the head of the pump is only 2.3ft (0.7m). Exceed this height and no solution, or very little, will leave the fountainhead at the top of the hose. Making it a lot less will result in a tall fountain. Using the height of the solution in the tank above the pump gives the grower control over the flow from the fountainhead; it has the effect of changing the head of the pump and should be used to give the desired flow of solution leaving the top of the pipe. If the grower starts with a level of solution that will give a good flow (a small fountain), then as the plants use water and nutrients the level will fall and the flow will be reduced. Add more solution of

Strawberry tree components.
Note the plastic nuts and bolts
at the bottom of the photo.

the same mix to restore the original flow. The rate of flow is not critical as long as the filter resting on the plastic bolt heads combined with the porosity of the medium used can pass the solution without flooding the unit. The minimum flow should maintain the medium in a damp state.

7. Fit the pump into the base of the soil pipe and connect the pipe from the fountainhead to the output of the pump. Check that the switch on the side of the pump is set for maximum flow.

8. Secure the three 3in (7.6cm) lengths of plastic pipe that are secured to the soil pipe to three sides of the tank using three more plastic nuts and bolts. This secures the 2ft 4in (71cm) soil pipe vertically in the water tank.

9. Now make a lip for each planting hole. Cut a piece of 1.6in (4cm) outside diameter plastic pipe into 2in (5cm) lengths. Slice each piece into two sections lengthways. Shape the two pieces as shown in the photo. It looks like a rounded tongue with a clip at each side on the rear. These 2in (5cm) lengths form the lips. Squeeze each across its width with pliers while holding it upwards at an angle of 45 degrees. Insert one into each planting hole and push it in. Quick-grips may be required. Release the pressure across its width and the plastics will spring open, gripping the sides of the planting hole while the clips will clip on to the inside of the Marley soil pipe.

10. Placing epoxy resin right round the underside of the lip will secure them to the Marley soil pipe and make a seal. These lips are required, as some plants (like strawberries) do not like the neck of the plant to be wet, and also the solution is prevented from running down the

The shape of the lip for the strawberry tree.

The completed strawberry tree.

outside of the tree. The plants rest on these lips with the roots in the medium.

11. Runners from the strawberry plants can be set into a plastic cup containing a little moist Rockwool. Later, when fully rooted, cut them away from the plant and place them in the tree holes.

12. The next step is to place the plants in the tree. Pre-soak the perlite and baked clay balls in the solution to be used for twelve hours. Remove as much dry medium as possible from the roots, then hold the plant close to the root system while moving the roots up and down in warm water 77°F (25°C) to remove the rest.

13. Using a mixture of one part Perlite to three parts baked clay balls, place a layer of the pre-soaked medium on the filter in the soil pipe up to the level of the first planting hole. Put the first layer of plants in position, avoiding air pockets around the roots. Cover the roots with more medium and continue up the soil pipe, planting in this way. Avoid leaving any air pockets around the roots. The coarse nature of the medium ensures that oxygen is available to the roots, but moisture must be available also.

14. If the medium is washed into position using a watering can with a full-strength solution and the tank emptied a few times, then the chance of air pockets being left around the roots is reduced. This procedure also washes a lot of the dust off the medium. Good drainage is very important.

A strawberry runner being rooted in moist Rockwool.

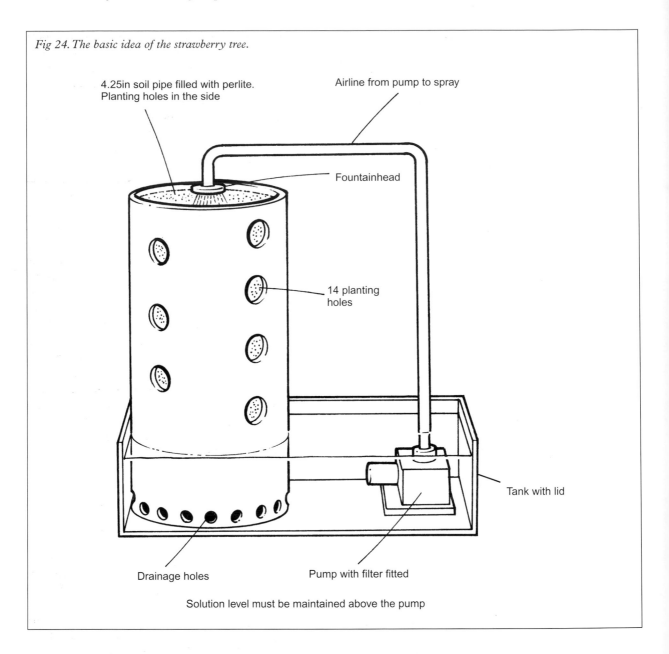

Fig 24. The basic idea of the strawberry tree.

4.25in soil pipe filled with perlite.
Planting holes in the side

Airline from pump to spray

Fountainhead

14 planting holes

Tank with lid

Drainage holes

Pump with filter fitted

Solution level must be maintained above the pump

15. When the planting is complete, make a mound of baked clay balls over the fountainhead; put some perlite around the mound of baked clay balls and plant some more flowers or strawberry plants around the top of the soil pipe. The growing medium must be kept moist, but equally important flooding must be avoided.

If the intention is to grow flowers with artificial light in a cool area, a small glass aquarium heater can be placed in the solution, heating it to 71.6°F (22°C.). If a heater is fitted, ensure that it does not come into contact with the plastic tank at any point. Clean house tiles placed between the heater and the plastic can perform this function. Make sure that there is good insulation between the tank and a cold floor. Extra care must be taken to see that the solution level does not fall too far. If the heater is taken out of the solution while hot, the heater glass will crack. As with any electrical equipment operating in water, fit a 30mA trip unit in the circuit and the appropriate size fuse in line with each item.

If the tank is made larger, then by using an air pump (4W) to inject air into the solution via a ceramic air stone (from a hydroponic supplier), the solution can be kept moving and aerated. This may be necessary with a large tank, as the solution is only recirculating within the base and top of the growing chamber. The solution in the tank could become stagnant as it is only maintaining the supply to the pump.

Any maintenance on the pump to clean the filter fitted in its base only requires removing the three plastic bolts and lifting out the Marley soil pipe complete with the plants and pump.

AEROPONICS

Aeroponic systems can be an ideal way to produce plants in the home ready for placing on hydroponic NFT trays. Good, clean plants with well-formed root systems are required for NFT work. The grower can start the plants in the home and have them ready for the greenhouse when the weather improves. Peas and beans can be grown to maturity using this system. In fact, most plants can be grown by aeroponics, even pineapples and pumpkins. The high level of oxygen in the solution required in an aeroponics system can be achieved by misting or air injection via an air stone.

A novel and effective means of providing the air and nutrients around the roots while at the same time heating the solution and aerating it is by using an ultrasonic wave atomizer. This generates a mist round the roots. The unit is raised up on a stand inside the solution container so that it is just below the surface of the solution.

The plant with its roots hanging down is suspended into the solution, so that the tips of the roots are just in the solution. The mist produced by the ultrasonic wave atomizer ensures that the roots above the solution are in a mist of nutrient and air.

In this experiment, the running cost of the atomizer was not high, but the high wattage (18W) is higher than an air pump (6W), which was found to do the job just as well. However, the atomizer was extremely successful. The high wattage did tend to increase the temperature of the solution in a container holding 35 pints (20l) and this helped with root growth. The high oxygen content of the nutrient solution must be maintained right through the growing period of the plant.

A good aeroponic unit can be made using a small plastic water tank or even a toy container. If the unit is to be sited in the home, the size will depend on

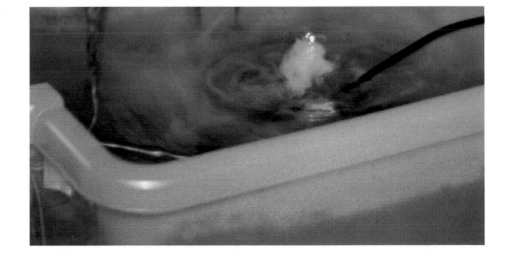

Mist effect produced by the ultrasonic atomizer.

Lid of the aeroponic atomizer unit lifted up to show the healthy roots.

The healthy root system of an aeroponic flower plant.

the space available on a windowsill or another suitable surface. Choose a spot with good light (natural or artificial) and with warmth.

Make a wooden frame to fit round the top of the tray. Stretch and attach a plastic mesh firmly over it to give the plant support. Peas or beans are a good first plant to grow, so place a large number of peas or bean seeds on perlite in a plastic plant pot, cover with more perlite, and keep moist. Remove the seedlings from the plastic plant pots when the first leaves appear. Wash off the perlite in warm water and insert the taproot through holes that have been made by stretching a hole in the plastic mesh. Fit a ceramic air stone on the output of a good air pump and place the air stone on the base of the container in the solution (if the tank is wide use two air stones and a pump with two outputs). Maintain the level of the solution in the container. Warming the solution to around 68°F (20°C) improves the root growth. If the plants are required for NFT systems, they can be cut out of the plastic mesh and the bare roots placed on the NFT tray when the root systems are seen to be good enough. Plants that are to continue growing in the system must be provided with ample air space for the foliage. Care must be taken not to damage the stems.

The toy container used in this experiment had a wooden frame made to fit over the top. Plastic mesh was stretched over the frame and the tray filled with

The roots of the bean plants in a hydroponic solution. The netting on a frame supporting the plants is reflected below. (The air pump was switched off to take this photo.)

Small pumpkin plants in a pot.

A tomato plant shares the aeroponic unit with a pumpkin plant and a potato plant.

Aeroponic Pumpkins

For larger plants such as pumpkins and tomatoes use Corribord for the lid of the container instead of plastic mesh (Corribord is sold by hydroponic stores). Cut holes in the Corribord lid to take the small net-like plant containers and fill the container with a hydroponic mix of cF12. Cut away the base of the net-like containers to allow the roots to hang through. If necessary, the plants can be attached to these containers. Fit the air pump and force the air through a ceramic air stone to give good aeration. A number of pumpkin seeds were started in a plant pot with vermiculite and perlite. When one of the pumpkin plants was around 2in (5cm) tall its root system was placed in one of the holes, a tomato plant in another and a shoot of a potato in another. The unit was then kept in a warm area in good light during the late winter.

The pumpkin or squash is well worth growing for its culinary uses. Nothing is wasted; even the seeds of the pumpkin can be used and are an excellent source of iron and phosphorus, as well as being rich in potassium, magnesium and zinc. The pumpkin flesh itself is a good source of beta-carotene and vitamin E. The human body converts the beta-carotene into vitamin A.

a weak hydroponic solution around cF8. Runner bean plants were hung through the mesh, with two-thirds of the length of the bare root system of the seedlings in the solution. The air pump was switched off to take the photograph on page 103, then put back on again.

Do not cut the plastic mesh, but widen a hole in it so that the roots of the plants can be dropped through the resulting hole, leaving the plant suspended by the foliage.

A still-green pumpkin rests in an old fish net.

The healthy white roots of the pumpkin as it was taken out of the system.

The mature aeroponic pumpkin; next stop, the table.

In this particular experiment, a pumpkin was grown aeroponically at the same time as one was started in the garden. Potatoes and tomatoes were also grown in the aeroponic system. In the spring, the aeroponic system was moved out into the greenhouse. This pumpkin attained a height of 6.6ft (2m), but was only permitted one fruit. By early July, the pumpkin in the greenhouse was a golden yellow and ready for cutting, whereas the pumpkin plant placed in the garden soil was just starting to produce flowers, despite the fact that both pumpkin plants had started life from seed at the same time.

The solution in the hydroponic unit remained

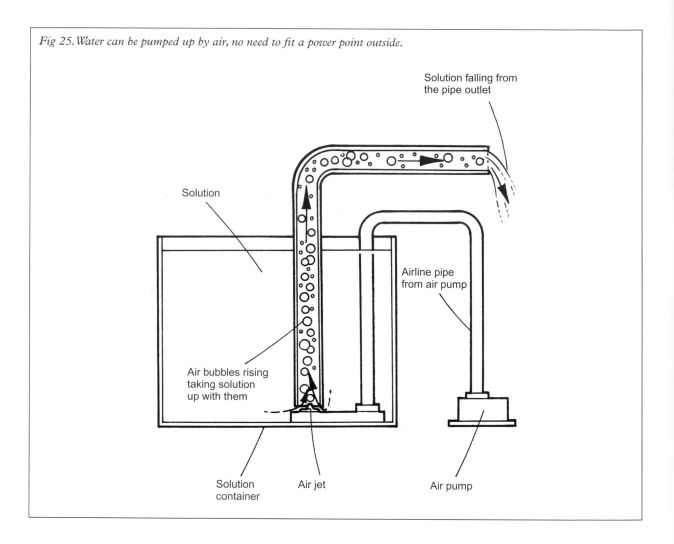

Fig 25. Water can be pumped up by air, no need to fit a power point outside.

Solution falling from
the pipe outlet

Solution

Airline pipe
from air pump

Air bubbles rising
taking solution
up with them

Solution
container

Air jet

Air pump

fairly constant at around 68°F (20°C) while it was in the warm area, but in the greenhouse it was more like 50°F (10°C).

The potato plant produced small potatoes; the tomato plant produced five very large tomatoes. Of course, the pumpkin produced only the one pumpkin.

AIR PUMPS

The outlet from an air pump is taken down through the solution, where the air is released into the base of a tube that has a larger diameter than the airline. The larger diameter tube has its outlet above the tank and extends to the deepest part of the tank. Air bubbles rising in the larger diameter pipe will force the solution up the pipe.

Air Pumps and Uses

There can be situations where problems arise, such as providing a correctly fitted 240V AC supply to an external point out of doors. This can be both difficult and expensive. If a mains-operated air pump is plugged into a convenient power outlet in a dry area, the pump will be dry and no extra wiring will be required. It can then be an easy matter to run an airline from the pump outlet to the area where the hydroponic system is to operate. The air-

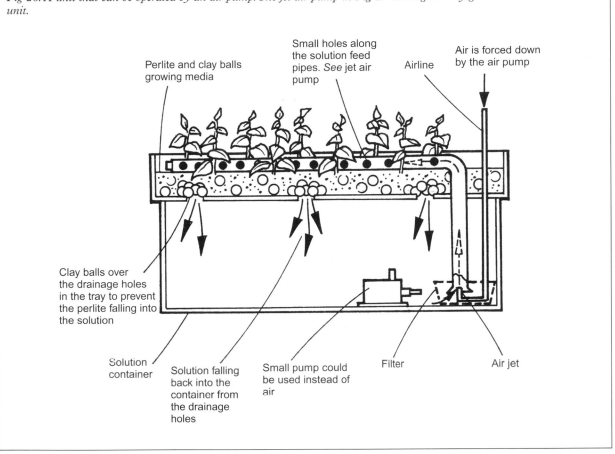

Fig 26. A unit that can be operated by an air pump. The jet air pump in Fig 27 would give very good results in this unit.

Perlite and clay balls growing media

Small holes along the solution feed pipes. *See* jet air pump

Airline

Air is forced down by the air pump

Clay balls over the drainage holes in the tray to prevent the perlite falling into the solution

Solution container

Solution falling back into the container from the drainage holes

Small pump could be used instead of air

Filter

Air jet

lines can be 10yd (9m) long or even longer using a good air pump. The air from this can then be used to pump the solution up on to the tray of a hydroponic unit.

The air pump must, of course, be able to force the air to the deepest part of the tank; this is where a good air pump is required. A mail order hydroponic supplier will advise. The best lift of water or solution is achieved with a good pressure of air and a good depth of water.

Using an Air-Injection Pump

The system described below is an NFT system. The pump is an air-injection pump. A normal air pump produces a stream or a trickle from the out-

let; this pump produces at intervals a small quantity of solution as a jet from each outlet in the feed pipe. The tank and tray can be made of UPVC, polypropylene or fibreglass, or a plastic storage box could be used. This design requires:

- a large plastic cup or bowl (to be called 'the vessel' in the construction instructions below), which is to act as the air reservoir
- one length of plastic pipe, 0.63in (1.6cm) internal diameter by around 39in (1m) long (bought from a hardware shop)
- a 90-degree bend to join two lengths of this pipe together
- one bung or end stop for this pipe
- a length of airline with an internal diameter to

plug on to the pump outlet; it also needs to be long enough to connect the NFT system with the air pump

- a solution container that will hold a depth of solution greater than 9in (23cm) and have a fitted lid
- a plastic tray just smaller than the solution container.

As this air pump is mains-operated, it needs to be fitted in a dry position. To prevent solution siphoning back into the pump, it should be placed higher than the injection air pump in the NFT system and have a one-way valve fitted.

Construction

This air pump is based on the normal air-pump idea but employs an air reservoir, which gives an injection of solution across the width of the tray at intervals instead of a constant trickle at one point.

1. Cut a hole in the vessel top to take the 0.63in (1.6cm) internal diameter pipe (this should be a good fit and have a length to suit the depth of solution).
2. Make a hole in the side close to the open end of this vessel to allow the large diameter airline to pass through. The airline must have an internal diameter to match the air pump's outlet, be a good fit in the vessel and have a length that allows the air pump and the solution pump to be connected.
3. Cut the end off this airline at an angle of 45 degrees before fitting into the base of the vessel. This angle cut should leave the airline longest at the bottom edge of the vessel. The vessel will form an air reservoir. The size of this vessel will determine the frequency of the ejection of the solution through the feed holes. Use a waterproof epoxy resin to seal and make an airtight joint between the riser pipe and the top of the vessel and seal the point where the airline enters the bottom of the vessel in the same way. The vessel when fitted in the system will have this riser pipe extending to above the NFT tray and the airline going into what is the base of the

vessel (reservoir) placed on the lowermost part of the main solution tank.
4. Fit the riser pipe from the vessel into one end of the 90-degree bend; fit the other end of it into the feed pipe, which is almost as wide as the NFT tray, being 10.5in (26.7cm), has eight holes 0.125in (3.2mm) drilled along the lower part of its length and an airtight plug fitted into the end. It is, of course, fitted above the highest end of the NFT tray. The tray is 15in long × 11.5in wide (38cm × 29cm) and has a slope of 4in (10cm) over the 15in (38cm) length. A benefit could be gained by increasing this slope slightly to give good drainage. The outlet of the air pump is fed directly into the base of the vessel – no air stone is needed. The tray could have large or small corrugations depending on the plants the grower wishes to grow.

The Pump Operation

Air from the air pump fills the upturned vessel, compressing the solution in the riser pipe; air escapes from the holes drilled in the feed pipe and the air in the vessel (reservoir) rises in the riser pipe, forcing the solution up into the feed pipe where some of it runs out of the 0.125in (3.2mm) holes drilled along its length on to the NFT tray. As the feed holes are in the lower part of the feed pipe, a small amount of solution remains, filling the outlet holes. The air and the solution from the riser pipe cannot escape until the pressure in the riser pipe is sufficient to force out the small amount of solution obstructing the feed holes. When the pressure builds up in the riser pipe (this occurs about once a second) the solution is ejected onto the NFT tray equally across the width of the tray via the 0.125in (3.2mm) feed holes.

Growing a Pineapple Plant

Enjoy a fresh pineapple and keep the top; it will grow into a pineapple plant given time, and with patience and persistence pineapples can be produced. It may take two to three years to get fruit from that plant, but if a greenhouse is available for the required time the pineapple plant could grow to around 6ft high × 6ft wide (1.83m × 1.83m) and produce good-sized fruit.

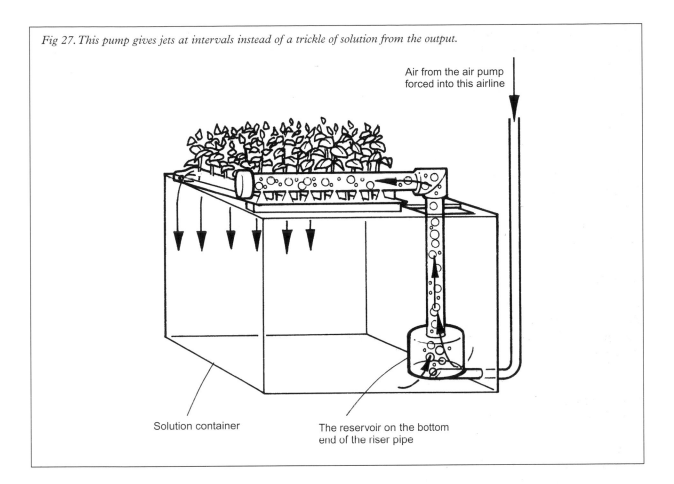

Fig 27. This pump gives jets at intervals instead of a trickle of solution from the output.

Air from the air pump forced into this airline

Solution container

The reservoir on the bottom end of the riser pipe

Pineapples grow on the top of the plant. When buying a pineapple, pick one with a healthy looking top. A fruit with loose leaves in the centre of its growing tip or with leaves in poor condition will not be fresh enough to produce a growing plant. A pineapple with some of the larger leaves in poor condition could be fine as long as the centre leaves are firm and fresh. Having found such a fruit and enjoyed it, prepare to make the top of it grow roots.

1. Remove the vegetation from the fruit cutting just below the last lower leaves. Remove the lower leaves to expose 0.5in to 0.75in (1.3cm to 1.9cm) of core by pulling them downwards and removing them in the growing order. The roots appear from the intersections with the core where the leaves have been.

2. To maintain moisture and air around the point where the leaves have been removed, split two small Rockwool cubes down the grain, and with a wire tie attach these four pieces of Rockwool (with the grain running vertically from top to bottom) around the base of the pineapple core. Place the pineapple top with the four Rockwool pieces around its base in a jar, which should have a diameter wide enough to be able to take the Rockwool pieces with the foliage of the pineapple top and allow the core to sit on the base. Add around 0.5in (1.3cm) of tepid water to the jar. Any fruit or decomposable particles that remain will foul the water in the jar, so this tepid water should be changed frequently over the next three to four weeks. The jar and plant head should be placed in good light in a warm room. Around three to four weeks later, roots

An alternative aeroponic unit can be set up using a two-output air pump.

should appear where the intersections of the old leaves have been.

3. At this point, aeroponics comes into play. In the experiment being described here, an aeroponic unit was constructed out of a dark green plastic bin fitted with a lid and with a capacity of 31.7 pints (18l). When the roots had formed around the base of the head, the Rockwool was carefully removed from around the roots and the plant was suspended in a hole in the lid with the tip of the roots just in the solution.

4. This system used an ultrasonic wave atomizer TC2420 in the container, which was filled with a hydroponic solution strength cF14; this gave good aeration.

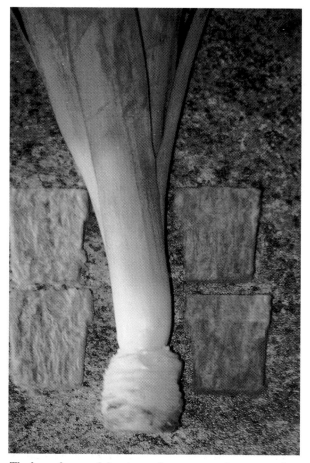

The lower leaves of the pineapple are removed to expose the core.

The core of the pineapple top is kept moist by four pieces of Rockwool.

Mist around the roots of the pineapple top generated by the ultrasonic wave atomizer.

Head of the pineapple top developing.

5. The container used held 31.7 pints (18 litres) of solution and as the ultrasonic wave atomizer consumed 13.2W of power at 240V, the heat applied to the solution produced temperatures in the region of 77°F (25°C); this was good for root growth. The TC2420 had the advantage over an air pump and an air stone of being very quiet. It could not be heard and the mist or vapour rising from it proved to be a talking point. The growing pineapple top approved of the temperature and produced a good root system in the solution. After ten days in the system, the centre of the pineapple had grown a stem 3in (7.6cm) high with a cluster of small petal-like leaves on the top of the stem. The root system was large and white (a sign of healthy roots).

6. The next step was to maintain the water level. The solution was changed after four weeks. As winter was approaching and the plant required longer hours of daylight than that available in the UK, light from a 20W high-efficiency lamp under the control of a timer provided light until 10pm. Thirteen to fourteen hours of light a day were given from 1 October to improve growth. Growing the plant in a container with adequate impenetrable colouring (preferably black) would be the best choice. The reason for this is that light penetrating the container will produce algae in the solution and on the inside of the container. If a coloured container is all that is available, then cover it with black polythene. Algae consume nitrogen from the solution, but

Photo of the TC2420 (ultrasonic wave atomizer) attached to a plastic container.

A two-output air pump gave good results but did not generate so much heat in the solution.

When the plant is large enough an apple can be placed near the tip to induce flowering!

can also be a breeding ground for pests. The plant (cutting) has blue-green foliage and a huge root system.

When the plant has made sufficient growth to support a small pineapple, possibly in the second or third year, flowering should commence. It is said that the following methods can be used to force pineapple plants into flowering. Hanging a ripe apple at the tip of the plant will release ethylene gas, which could make it flower; this sounds a reasonably safe way. It was found in New Zealand many years ago that by placing a ripe apple in with Kiwi fruit, they would ripen. The ethylene gas is reputed to work with pineapple plants also. Apparently laying the plant and pot on its side in between watering can upset it enough to make it flower; maybe it is a form of seasickness! The other method is a small lump of calcium carbide placed in the tip of the plant with a small quantity of water dripped on to the calcium carbide. This produces acetylene gas and a lot of white calcium paste/powder. However, if time and the right growing conditions are available, then when the plant is large enough it will know what to do. Warm solution temperatures are important. Aim for 61°F to 77°F (16°C to 25°C) and, of course avoid frost on the foliage at all costs.

The pineapple flowers are light blue to purple. They start from the bottom and open row by row. When the last flowers have died, the fruit starts to develop.

A Group of Pineapples

A group of pineapples, one of which was a micro-pineapple, was planted in an Anthea planter (from a hydroponic store) designed as a neat window box. The medium used was a mixture of perlite and vermiculite fed with hydroponic nutrients. All plants in the system did well. This planter has a tray clipped on to its base to hold the run-off solution as the planter is fed from above. The solution is in contact with air and the level can be seen through a slot.

Cucumbers in an Aeroponic Unit

Before beginning this experiment, the cucumber seeds were planted in perlite soaked in water and placed in a spot with warmth and good light. The strongest seed was allowed to grow and when the plant was around 3in (7.6cm) high it was transferred to the aeroponic system after having the perlite washed from the roots.

The following items are required:

- an old music CD of any sort or an old personal computer CD
- a small plant pot around 3in (7.6cm) in diameter
- one 0.8in (2cm) open cable grommet

Provide good light in a warm, frost-free area, and in two to three years it could produce another pineapple.

An Anthea planter from a hydroponic store containing a group of pineapple plants.

Lid of the container lifted up to show the root system filling the container.

- a good air pump – one with two outputs would be an advantage if a larger container were to be used, as this would spread the aeration over a larger area
- one or two ceramic air stones with rubber sucker attachment supplied; the number of air stones will depend on the pump (double or single outlet)
- a length of airline long enough to enable the air pump (sited in a dry place) to be connected to a ceramic air stone positioned in the growing container; if an air pump with two outlets feeding two air stones is used, then two lengths of airline will be required
- one solution-growing container – the size will depend upon the area available. In this experiment, the dark green bread bin with a lid that had been used in the past was available; it had a capacity of 15.8 pints (9l).

System construction

1. Cut a hole in the lid of the container to allow the plant pot to hang into it suspended by its rim.
2. Cut the base of the plastic plant pot out (leave a rim on to keep the plant pot in shape). A pair of old scissors will do for the entire cutting procedure.
3. Make the small hole in the middle of the CD larger – around 1.1in (2.8cm) in diameter.

4. Cut a 0.47in (1.2cm) slot into the CD (from the outside of the CD to one side of the hole in the middle).
5. Place the normally open end of the plant pot on top of the CD, and after drawing around the plant pot cut the CD so that it fits into the top of the plant pot.
6. Take the 0.8in (2cm) cable grommet and make one cut in it so that it can be opened larger than 0.8in (2cm). Place this grommet around the 1.1in (2.8cm) hole cut in the CD. Have the open end of the grommet so that the slot cut into the CD remains open. It may require a spot of epoxy resin to secure the grommet in position. This is to cater for the expansion of the plant stem. As the plant grows the stem can reach 1.1in (2.8cm) in diameter.

Establishing the plant

1. Place the plant in the plant pot with the roots hanging through the base.
2. Fill the plant pot very loosely with a peat substitute around the stem of the plant. Arrange the plant so that all the root system is below the base of the plastic pot.
3. Twist the CD gently, making the slot in it wider and slide it (reflective side up) around the stem of the plant with the grommet in position

Construction of the cucumber unit.

around the hole that has just been enlarged. The grommet will protect the plant's stem from the sharp edges of the new hole in the CD; the CD will reflect light on to the plant.

4. This should leave the plant with its roots hanging out of the base of the plant pot and the plant stem supported in position. Place both the plant and plant pot into the hole in the lid of the container with the roots hanging through the pot base.

5. The container is now filled with a hydroponic solution (cF14) to a height that covers 0.75in (1.9cm) of the root system. The solution level can be raised in stages as the plant grows. The level of this solution is maintained by adding water and the strength by adding nutrients or by replacing the solution used by more of the same cF.

High aeration is very important in the form of lots of small air bubbles. A good air pump and a ceramic air stone achieve the aeration; these can be obtained by mail order from hydroponic suppliers. The air pump used in this system has two outlets to feed two air stones. Connect the air pump to a 240V outlet, join the air pump and the air stone together using the airline, and attach the air stone to the base of the container with the rubber sucker

The cucumber plant waiting to be moved into position.

The cucumber plant trained over the outside of the garage window.

The cucumber plant.

supplied. Have the pump running for the full twenty-four hours per day. The leafy shoots were trained over the outside of the garage window in a cordon form.

In this experiment, the plant with a crop of thirty thirsty cucumbers consumed 3.52 pints (2l) of water a day. In view of this high demand, it would have been more practical to have used a growing container with a capacity of around 35.2 pints (20l). The small growing container could have been topped up from a mains source under the control

of a float valve, and then the cF would have been easily maintained manually.

It was important to ensure that the system received its top-up water as the number and size of the cucumbers grew. This was administered through a funnel directly into the container.

As the plant grows and its roots fill the container, the level of the solution can be raised to cover all the root system. Avoid raising the solution so high that it overflows. This will just waste nutrients, which will have to be replaced.

FEED ON DEMAND

The system described here is ideally suited to growing cuttings and plants required for NFT work; the medium is easily removed and good white bare roots are achieved. Small plants are likely to be in the system for a long time and can be looked after automatically during holiday periods. Tomatoes or cucumbers can be grown to maturity in an area with good light and heat.

As moisture is drawn from the medium due to evaporation or by the demands of the plants, the system replaces the solution (nutrients and water). This system does this without the use of timing

Large number of cucumbers developing.

devices or power. By harnessing atmospheric pressure coupled with hydroponics it gives free automatic operation. Large plants will appreciate the addition of a small 4W air pump and a ceramic air stone.

The Theory of the System

A strong airtight container full of solution but with a hole in its base will not release any solution at all from this hole after a vacuum has formed in the top. The vacuum will hold the solution in against gravity, but as soon as air is allowed (by any means) into the top of the container, solution will flow from that hole. This fact can be used to produce a system that will maintain the residual level of solution in a growing tray automatically.

The self-feed hydroponic unit as constructed.

The first and most important point is that the solution container and any feed-offs must be absolutely airtight. The second is that this container must be strong enough to prevent it collapsing inwards when submitted to an internal vacuum. A very small amount of implosion of the container due to the internal vacuum can be accepted and expected, but if the container used cannot stand the vacuum and the sides are pulled in, loss of capacity along with poor control of the feed (overwatering) can result.

If the grower intends using a recycled carboy for the solution container, it must be given a very good clean before use. Any carboys that have transported pesticides should be rejected. The size of the container (carboys or similar) should be adjusted to suit the plants, the time that the solution is to last and the area in which they are to be sited.

Items Required

- A length of clear plastic pipe 0.75in (22mm) internal diameter. This is the solution feed pipe. This is required to pass feed from the solution container into the base of the growing container.
- A length of clear plastic pipe just smaller in out-

The detachable growing unit planted with a cucumber plant. Airlines feed the ceramic air stone in the residual solution in the base.

side diameter than the internal diameter of the 0.75in (22mm) pipe. This is the air feed pipe and should extend from the very top of the airtight solution contained down to its base and out into the solution container to the height in the growing container of the required residual solution. It is important that this is all in one piece.

• A straight tank connector as used in cold-water overflow systems, 0.75in (22mm) in size.
• Two containers (one able to withstand a vacuum).

System Construction

1. A straight tank-fitting 0.75in (22mm) is fitted into a hole drilled in one side of the base of the solution container. To fit this tank-fitting in the base, remove the screw top from the container

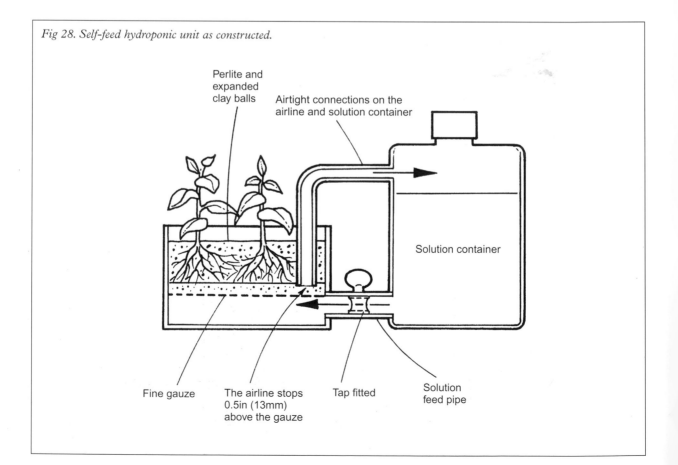

Fig 28. Self-feed hydroponic unit as constructed.

Perlite and expanded clay balls

Airtight connections on the airline and solution container

Solution container

Fine gauze

The airline stops 0.5in (13mm) above the gauze

Tap fitted

Solution feed pipe

and feed a length of wire tie into the container; a pair of long-nose pliers can be used to pull the wire tie from inside the container through the hole intended for the tank-fitting.

2. After coating the tank-fitting and washers with a liberal coating of silicon sealant, thread them on the wire tie protruding from the screw top on the top of the container.

3. Place the end of the tank-fitting that is to protrude from the hole in the container base so that it will travel down the wire and enter the container first. Make the wire end secure at the top and allow the tank-fitting to slide along the wire inside the container, fishing it into position through the hole drilled into the container base using long-nose pliers.

4. Then put the plastic washer and nut on with more sealant and tighten to make a seal. Remove the wire tie. Check that the tank-fitting will enter the hole before starting this procedure.

5. Heat a length of large diameter clear plastic hose in very hot water and push it on the outlet of the tank-fitting; a jubilee clip and more silicon sealant will complete this end of the job.

6. The air pipe (another clear plastic pipe just able to fit through the large diameter pipe connected between the solution container and the growing container) is now threaded through the large diameter plastic pipe and fished out of the screw top on the top of the solution container (turning the container upside-down

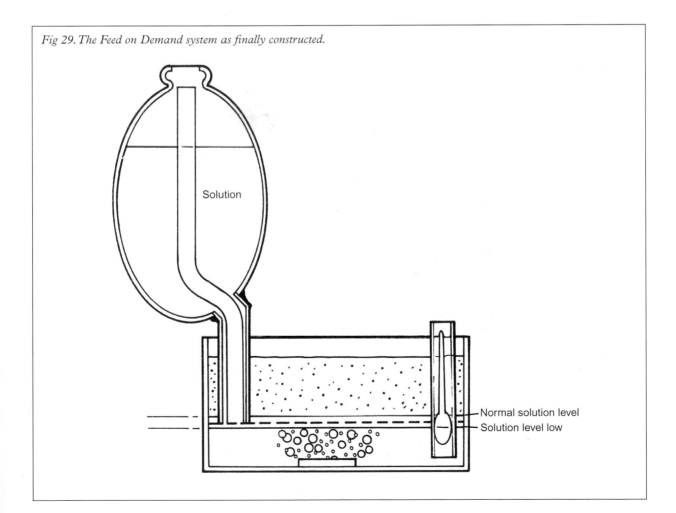

Fig 29. The Feed on Demand system as finally constructed.

Solution

Normal solution level
Solution level low

makes this easier). String will secure this temporarily in the top of the container and a shaped wine cork will hold it in its permanent position below the screw top. When the container is filled, solution is able to feed between the clear air pipe and the larger-diameter clear solution pipe, as again algae will grow on the inside of this tube.

7. Attach two ceramic air stones securely to the base of the growing container after connecting them to a two-output air pump.

8. Fill the growing container with a hydroponic solution at the cF and pH required.

9. The solution container with its trunk can be removed from one growing container and moved to another, giving flexibility of use.

10. Suspend the plant with its bare roots (no medium at all) in the solution so that the solution covers all the root system of the plant.

The system is extremely well suited to aeroponic systems such as growing an aeroponic cucumber, and is equally well suited to topping up units like the orange tree, both described in previous pages. With a good size Feed on Demand container the areoponic system can be left unattended for very long periods at a time.

Perlite should be avoided in the aeroponic system as it floats to the surface, reducing the area of solution in contact with air. Light falling onto the solution will introduce algae into the solution. If plastic is used to prevent light or dust entering the solution, it must be suspended high above the solution to allow air to flow over the surface area; this is another source of oxygen for the solution and the plant roots. Gasses produced by the roots must be allowed to disperse.

NB: The Feed on Demand system is the subject of a patent; anyone wishing to produce it commercially should contact the author via The Crowood Press.

CHAPTER 8

Making a Low-Cost Unit to Compare cF Readings

The construction of this comparison cF meter is very simple. Basically it involves converting a commercially designed unit to do another task. This requires the removal of two components and replacing them with four wires. The ability to use a small-tipped soldering iron is required.

Each meter constructed (module modified) can give a hand-held means of comparing the cF with a solution of a known cF. Automatic control of the cF requires the construction of a unit, along with additional items for each system (or each tank) in use. The module, based on a commercial unit designed as a digital thermometer, costs around £17 in total for the manual version including all the components. It measures temperatures to within 0.1°C and is sold by Maplin Electrical Suppliers (Maplin code FP64U). The module can be made to perform many tasks, is battery-operated, has a large digital read-out and is far superior to a reading displayed by a needle passing over a scale.

Automatic control of the cF in a system requires the basic unit with the addition of a relay and two liquid valves for each tank. One correctly rated power supply will feed a number of relays if required. The basic unit with the addition of a transistor, relays and a power supply can automatically control a fan heater and a cooling fan or the lighting.

The completed meter (module) can be calibrated against a test solution purchased from a hydroponic supplier. After calibration, the reading given by the module when the probe is placed in the new solution will be noted and compared with the reading given by the test solution. Both solutions must be at the same temperature.

When the module is in operation, the probe is immersed in the return tank (main tank) giving readings continuously; it can then be seen at a glance if the tank solution is lower than the cF required. By adding equal quantities of concentrated stock solutions A and B to the tank or a

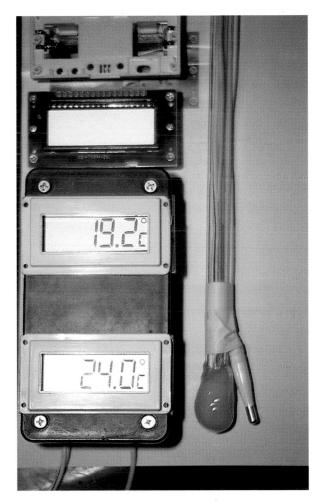

Three modules, one with the battery holder removed. Platinum cF probe and temperature sensor alongside.

quantity of a single mix of liquid concentrate, the cF can be made up to or returned to the value required.

A switch fitted in the circuit will enable the unit to give readings in either Fahrenheit or Celsius. The external temperature probe (Maplin code FP65V) is only required for duties involving temperatures. The items quoted here can be obtained by mail order from Maplin if they cannot be obtained locally.

MODULE DETAILS

- The calculations on the modules are based on the resistance of probes or devices fitted to it on two wires named A and B.
- The module operates from a 1.5V AA cell mounted behind the LCD.
- The total current for the module is around 10μA.
- The display figures are 0.5in (1.3cm) high.
- When the unit has been modified the module can record and display the highest and lowest comparisons of cF values attained since it was reset.
- A number can be set for the minimum value of cF of the solution required in the tank. The module will give 1.5V out on pin 7 when the solution cF falls below this minimum number and an automatic function can be triggered. This voltage remains on pin 7 for a minimum of one minute or until the set number is exceeded. The minimum value can be changed as many times as required.
- The unit has lots of other facilities, but pin 7 is the only one used for the cF version. To make use of the output from the pins on the module for automatic operation three switches are required. These switches will be of the type that will be electrically closed only while held pressed.

It is important to note that if the module is in automatic cF injection mode, the probe must be immersed in the solution at all times, otherwise it will register the cF as low and operate the liquid valves. For the basic cF meter the switches are not required but the pins are always available for a future date.

Using this module with the three switches fitted, the unit can automatically control the injection of solutions A and B with the assistance of two electrically operated low-pressure liquid valves, one relay and a power unit. A switch fitted and held

operated will connect the following pins together and permit this operation:

- between pins 16 and 5 will permit the module to display its currently set value for the low cF
- between pins 16 and 3 will permit the module to be set to the required low cF value
- between pins 16 and 11 will enable the module to display the highest or the lowest reading since the module was last reset, using pin 4 (high setting) and pin 5 (low setting).

See the manual issued with the module for further details.

If after setting up the display on the unit to read minimum 20 the reading falls to 19.9, a 1.5V DC charge will be put out on pin 7 that will switch on the transistor (BC183L Maplin code QB56L). This transistor will then feed power to the relay, which in turn can switch on the 12V or 24V DC to the two electrically operated valves. One liquid valve will control the concentrated solution A and the other will control the concentrated solution B. Concentrated solution from both valves will flow by gravity from the two containers A and B above the main tank, maintaining the reading on the display above 20 or the set number. When this has been achieved the two liquid valves will switch off and the flow will cease. If the grower's intention is to use the single concentrated mix of nutrients, then only one electrically operated liquid valve will be required.

As the module only takes 10μA it can be left switched on, taking readings continuously whilst operating a relay by way of a transistor. The module will last over a year on one good AA battery, but the relays, the two electrically operated liquid valves and the transistor will require an extra power supply.

The concentration of the top-up solutions A and B will have to be adjusted and the rate of flow (diameter of feed pipes) arranged, as this output remains on for a minimum of sixty seconds once it has switched off and on again. The concentrated nutrients from the A and B valves should be arranged to feed into the main tank a good distance apart.

MODIFYING THE MODULE UNIT

The following materials are required. A manual is supplied with the module.

- One min/max thermometer module. Maplin code FP64U.
- One 10k potentiometer UH25C, sold as '3/8in square 22 turns pre-set'. Two will be required in series if the grower decides to change from platinum to graphite probes.
- Tools – soldering iron (small bit) and cord solder.

Remove the cover from the unit along with the battery housing. Remove the small pinhead thermistor (temperature sensor) fitted to the right of a 4.7k ohm resistor and put this to one side for future use. This is shown in the manual. A hot small-tipped soldering iron is strongly recommended. *See* the soldering tips at the end of this chapter.

Solder two wires (called A and B) to the tags where the pinhead sensor has been. Wires A and B should be long enough and very flexible, not thick

and unwieldy as they will be connected to the probe.

Next remove the 4.7k resistor and extend the two connecting points left vacant by the resistor by soldering on another two wires C and D. These two wires will be taken to the pre-set potentiometers VR1 and, if fitted, VR2. These potentiometers are required to adjust the range of the unit. The value

Screwdrivers point out the resistor and pinhead thermistor to be removed and replaced by wires.

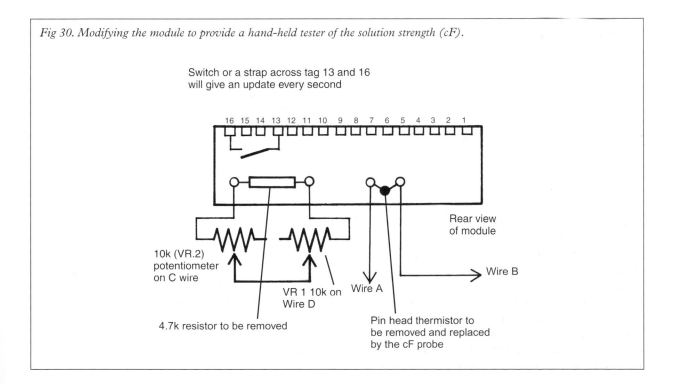

Fig 30. Modifying the module to provide a hand-held tester of the solution strength (cF).

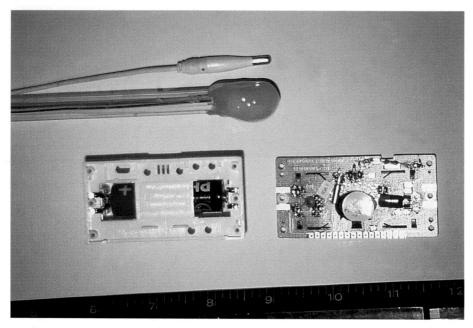

One module with the battery holder removed. Platinum tip probe and temperature sensor alongside.

of VR1 depends on the area of platinum (or, if used, drawing graphite) in contact with the solution. If graphite is used for the probe, a second resistor (VR2) could be required in series with VR1 to extend the module's adjustment range.

If a strap is soldered between pin 16 on the top of the module and pin 13, the module will update its readings every second. If this strap is not in position it will update the readings every fifteen seconds. The strap could be put in using a small switch for testing, switching into the fifteen-second mode for unattended operation. These are the only modifications to the module itself in its basic form.

Construction of the Probe

The materials required are:

- a glass tube similar to that used by winemakers, around 12in (30.5cm) long by 0.38in (1cm) diameter
- a length of platinum wire (used in some laboratory units) about 0.5in to 0.75in (1.3cm to 1.9cm) long; the longer length will be easier to solder on to the wire ends
- a length of twin flexible wire to connect the probe to the module

- epoxy resin adhesive rapid
- about thirty minutes of time, not counting waiting time.

The early probes were made using graphite drawing pencils with the plastic covering removed. While these were effective, they required more maintenance and so were superseded by the platinum wire probe. To make this probe, a glass tube 12in long by 0.38in (35.5cm by 1cm) wide is required. Take the two wires down the middle and solder two platinum wires around 0.25in to 0.5in (6.4mm to 1.3cm) long on to the ends of each. Epoxy resin is painted over the end of the glass tube and the wires with the platinum soldered on, allowing only the tip of the platinum wire to be in contact with the solution. This platinum probe gives good, reliable results and is cheap and easy to make. The end of the glass tube where the wires enter should be sealed with epoxy resin also.

Testing the Unit

1. Connect the two wires (A and B) from the module together. The unit with the battery fitted in should now flash HHH (for high). If it does not, check for continuity of the two wires.

2. Remove the connection between the two wires A and B and leave them open circuit and the unit should flash LLL (for low). If it does not, check the insulation between the two wires.

3. Connect the probe to the unit with the probe tip dry; the unit should flash LLL (for low). If it does not flash LLL, but instead gives a reading (with the probe dry and connected), then the insulation between the two electrodes in the probe is not very good and that will have to be cleared up before using that probe. This may be resolved by applying more epoxy resin (after drying out the probe) to prevent the solution getting into the glass tube of the probe, where it could remain, giving a reading.

Adjusting and Testing the Unit

1. Place the probe into a container (a large dish or something wider than a jam-jar) containing a test solution. A test solution can be obtained from hydroponic suppliers. Always have the base of the probe's electrodes with more than 1in (2.5cm) of solution below and around them.

2. Adjust the 22-turn potentiometer VR 1 (in conjunction with VR2 if fitted) with the probe in a test solution until a reading or figure is obtained which will represent the cF of that test solution to the grower. If the test solution is cF10, the reading could be made 10. It must be remembered the reading of 10 now obtained on the module is only a comparison reading. If thin graphite rods have been used to construct the probe in place of the platinum, then the two potentiometers in series will be required to give the range of readings that the grower requires.

3. If the grower needs to adjust VR1 frequently as cF readings are being taken in a number of systems set at different strengths, then Fig 31 (along with Fig 30) can be used. The required numbers of 22-turn potentiometers and probes can be switched into circuit using a rotary switch. Each combination of 22-turn potentiometers will have

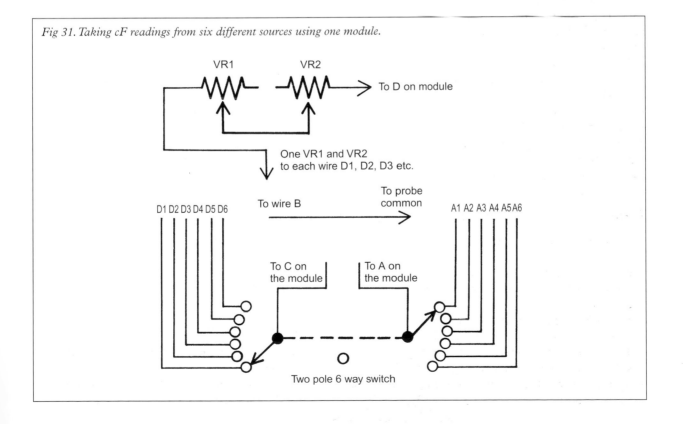

Fig 31. Taking cF readings from six different sources using one module.

to be adjusted with the associated probe in the appropriate solution.

If the grower can manage by noting the reading in each solution, then one module and one adjustment of VR1 is all that is required, saving a lot of extra work. (*See* also Fig 30.)

WHAT TO DO IF THE UNIT CRASHES

If the module crashes for any reason (the display goes off), remove the battery for a time, dry out the unit if needed, replace the battery and reprogram the settings. This module has been found to be very robust and reliable if care is taken with the construction. Like all electrical gear the module does not like very high humidity, but unless the grower actually sprays it, this should not be a problem. If the module does get damp the display will go off completely. To give some protection to the module, if it is exposed to high humidity place it in a clear plastic bag with a wire tie round where the wires enter.

If the solutions in the greenhouse are heated and controlled by a thermostat, then when the time comes to use the unit, temperatures will be reasonably steady. Under these conditions the temperature factor can be ignored.

The probe is left in the main tank night and day. This gives a constant update every second and at a given figure on the module the unit adds an equal number of millilitres of A and B to maintain the figure above the set number. For example, if the set figure is 20 then when the reading on the module falls to 19.9, concentrated solution will flow at a controlled rate until the reading is above 20 or for one-minute minimum. The flow will now cease until the reading falls below 20 again.

A pair of wires can be run to the probe with the module some distance away in a dry place if required. An extremely long cable between the probe and the module could give problems. The setting-up described above will have to be done with this extra wire in circuit. If the probe, or the distance to the probe, is changed then the whole adjusting procedure should be performed again.

The aim of all this is to have two pieces of platinum, with very good insulation between them that will allow only the platinum to be in contact with

the solution even after immersion in the solution for years. A plastic box can be used to contain the module and the resistors for the hand-held unit.

If the probes are to be permanently immersed (as against hand-held and inserted in the solution), then they should be suspended in the solution to a fixed depth. Do not have an air stone near the probe as the bubbles will upset the readings.

Maintenance

If graphite has been used for the electrodes rub the face of the graphite electrodes three or four times with a very fine grade wet and dry paper. All that is required for the platinum wire probe is a gentle brush now and then. Ensure that there are good soldered connections between the probe and the module at all points. Carry out tests from time to time with a cF standard solution.

THE CHANGE IN READINGS REPRESENTING THE cF DURING TEMPERATURE CHANGES

The true cF of the solution was cF20 for all the readings below.

Temperature	Small pin 1 × 0.9mm Graphite	Large pin 1 × 5mm Graphite	Platinum wire
16.1°C	19.1	18.5	31.1
16.2°C	19.3	18.6	31.1
16.4°C	19.3	19.0	31.2
16.7°C	19.6	19.3	31.3
17.0°C	19.8	19.4	31.6
17.1°C	20.0	19.6	31.8
17.4°C	**20.0**	**20.0**	**31.8**
18.0°C	20.4	20.5	32.2
18.4°C	20.5	20.9	32.4

The readings on the platinum pin probe could have been adjusted with VR1. The platinum pin probe had another use and so was not readjusted. The readings were adjusted on the modules while the small and the large pin probes were in a solution of cF20; the temperature of the solution was 63.3°F (17.4°C). The platinum pin probe and the small pin probe had no temperature compensation in circuit. The reading on the platinum probe was set at 31.8 with the solution at 63.3°F (17.4°C).

In tests carried out over four years, using two thicknesses of graphite and one platinum wire probe, the platinum wire-tipped probe and the large graphite probe proved to be the best, with the platinum coming first and the large graphite probe second. The module is shown on page 124 with the glass tube probe with 0.1in (2.5mm) of platinum wire protruding through the epoxy resin.

AVOIDING UNNECESSARY INJECTION OF NUTRIENTS IN AUTOMATIC MODE

If the module is to be used for the automatic control of the solution cF it is important that the solution temperature is maintained at a reasonably constant level, unless really good temperature compensation is used on the probe. If the minimum value is set on the module when the solution temperature has risen at midday, then when the temperature falls in the evening the cF will fall and could trigger an unnecessary cF injection.

To avoid this situation, the minimum value on the module should be set when the solution is at the minimum temperature set on the solution heating control.

The following will give some idea of the performance of the platinum probe and a modified module. With the probe in a solution of cF22 the reading was cF22. Without any further adjustment and with the probe in tap water the reading was cF–22. The cF of tap water in this area is cF2. Both solutions were at the same temperature.

Trouble may be experienced in obtaining the module (Maplin code FP64U) and its probe (code FP66W). However, the module (code FE 33L) and its probe (code FE34M) are good replacements; this module is cheaper but it cannot display the lowest and highest reading since it was last reset. Instead, it has a 12-hour clock display within the module and the extra facility of a serial data output. A futher output transmits the data clock. The transistor to replace the BC 182L/BC183 used in all the diagrams to convert the 1.5V into 240V AC is now BC337.

A FEW TIPS FOR SOLDERING

• Both parts of the joint must be at the same high temperature. Apply the tip of the iron to the point of contact between the wire end and the printed circuit board. Solder will flow only if both connections are clean and at a high temperature. After cleaning do not have any contact with the cleaned surface as oxide can form, giving a poor electrical connection. The component wire will be tinned, as will be the printed circuit board; do not clean these.

• A fairly high wattage iron is generally good with printed circuit board work; the heat need only be applied for a short time (two to three seconds at the most). Too long and it can do damage. Always start with a clean working area at the end of the soldering iron bit.

• Clean the copper bit with fine grade abrasive paper. Heat the iron to working temperature and apply a good standard 60 per cent tin, 40 per cent lead alloy solder with cores of non-corrosive flux built in. Wipe the tip of the iron with a damp sponge or cloth so that the solder forms a film over the copper bit (tinning it).

• To remove a component apply a dab of solder to the tinned copper face of the iron and while holding one wire of the component with a pair of long-nosed pliers bring the solder on the iron in contact with the soldered surface of that wire. Remove the component one wire at a time. It is the molten solder on the tip of the iron that allows the heat to flow to the joint. Do not keep the iron on the printed circuit board longer than necessary. If the iron has the right amount of solder on it, is hot and is placed correctly then the solder will flow.

• Apply the cord solder to the point where the copper track, soldering iron and wire to be soldered are touching each other. About one second is all that is needed. Take care not to put too much solder on the iron face as the solder may run on the printed circuit board, shorting out adjacent contacts.

Nature's World, Middlesbrough
Ecostructure' and 'Hydroponicum'

Fig 32. A hydroponicum is being constructed at Nature's World, Middlesbrough, in the UK. It is powered by solar energy and has geothermal heating. (Artist's drawing)

COMMERCIAL GROWERS

Visiting a commercial greenhouse growing tomatoes and cucumbers using hydroponic methods is amazing. Everything is big, very big, from the dimensions, to the amount of growth and the computerization. Holland has huge areas of greenhouses called 'glass cities'. There are vast hydroponic concerns in the UK as well.

Commercial growers grow tomato plants from seed in 3.5in × 3.5in × 2.5in (8.9cm × 8.9cm × 6.4cm) high blocks of Rockwool (a chemically inert material that offers a high air-to-nutrient content). When the plant is around 9in (23cm) high with good root systems and the roots have become adventurous, it is placed in contact with the medium in the bolster. The plastic of the bolster is cut for this. The bolsters for Rockwool are around 3ft long × 9in wide × 2.5in deep (91cm × 23cm × 6.4cm) and are covered in a plastic case. Six tomato plants are placed to a slab or bolster. Before the ini-

tial planting, the medium in the bolster or slab is saturated and soaked for twenty-four hours with a solution containing all the necessary growing elements required by the plant. Slots are then cut in the base of the plastic to allow all the excess solution to drain away. Solution at a constant cF and pH is applied by drip feed to the blocks containing the plants. As the surplus solution drains off, air is pulled into the medium, supplying both the oxygen and the nutrients required. This surplus is then allowed to run to waste or collected, treated and used again.

Feed to run-off is favoured commercially, as it is a lot easier to maintain the balance of the nutrients round the roots. Maintaining all the elements in the original balance along with oxygen around the roots is important.

Two Bezemer brothers have such a complex outside Stokesley in the north-east of England growing tomatoes and cucumbers. Their father came over from Holland in 1934. In 1947 he bought some

Commercial greenhouse, Stokesley, north-east England; note the roads rather than paths.

heavy land in Stokesley and after moving a lot of good fertilizer on to it and working it, he grew lettuce. Eventually, his sons moved into growing tomatoes and cucumbers hydroponically, as they found that growing these plants by traditional methods was proving uneconomical. They now grow tons and tons of tomatoes and cucumbers in greenhouses that have roads (not paths) down the centre and pack them under the name of 'English Villages'.

The greenhouses are so huge that they are split up into patches and given an address in the form of a name and two letters, as in a postcode. On one of the roadways leading to the exit there is a cluster of single instruments looking a bit like mobile phones.

Each one of these instruments has a keypad and a display. The grower working on the plants in the greenhouse takes one of these instruments along each time to report any potential problems that may require attention or if special tests are to be carried out. Information as to the condition of the plants, red spider or white fly and the like on the leaves is then keyed into the instrument along with the area code. This is then transmitted to a central unit, which sends it to the computer in the office where the appropriate action is taken.

The plants are grown in double rows spreading

out on each side of the roadways. Heating pipes run down one side of the plants looped at the end and back down the other side. At the bottom of that row they are looped again and run up one side of the next row and so on.

This is the same in the rows on both sides of the road. The central heating pipes are now on both sides of each row with a loop connecting them in series. Conveniently, they form railway lines running around 6in (15.2cm) above the ground in the centre of the plants so a trolley with rollers on is placed across the pipes.

The grower sits or stands on these to attend to the plants. Rockwool bolsters ready to take the plants are placed in the middle of the loop of central heating pipes without the trolley on.

The tomato plants themselves are planted in 3in (7.6cm) cubes of plastic-covered Rockwool; these are left open at the top and the bottom and the grain of the Rockwool itself runs downwards. When the roots have fully developed in the cube and the plant itself is the required height, the cube and plant are placed in contact with the pre-soaked Rockwool in the bolster. A hole is cut in the plastic of the bolster to facilitate this and a drip-feed unit is clipped into the top of the cube.

Solution is fed via the drip-feed unit into the

The units are used to report potential problems.

Heating pipes run down both sides of each row of plants.

cube at 25 to 30 per cent in excess of the plant's requirements, which then flows into the Rockwool of the bolster. Rockwool in the bolster had already been saturated with solution before the plants were put in position. The surplus is not presently recycled in this unit; in Holland, it is collected, cleaned, tested and used again.

Gas is burnt to heat the water in the central heating pipes in the boiler house outside. In this system, there are two methods for extracting the carbon dioxide. In the first method, the fumes are sucked out of the back of the boiler; they contain 11 per cent carbon dioxide and because the flame is not hot enough no nitrous oxide is produced, and as the

The heating pipes conveniently form railway lines; a trolley with rollers is placed on these.

A hole is cut in the plastic of the bolster and the contents of the cubes are placed in contact with the medium inside the bolster.

boiler is so efficient, there is also no carbon monoxide. Detectors on the back of the boiler provide a safety device preventing any toxic gases entering the greenhouse. The gases are blown into the greenhouse via a transparent plastic tube 3.5in (8.9cm) in diameter. Along the length of this tube 0.2in (5mm) holes are placed at intervals of 6in (15.2cm).

The second method of producing the carbon dioxide is a large heat and power station producing 4.5MW along with standby generators. The power station produces the 4.5MW and most of this is fed into the grid with a small amount used in the greenhouse. This unit also produces waste heat and carbon dioxide. The heat at around 194°F (90°C) is

The large clear plastic tube carries the carbon dioxide. The drip-feed pipe is in the top of each cube.

In one season the plant can grow 105ft (32m) parallel to the ground, plus 20ft (6m) up the wire.

used in the greenhouses as normal and the carbon dioxide is passed through a catalytic converter and fed round the greenhouse via the 3.5in (8.9cm) pipe. Gases being blown into the tube are either on or off; this operation is under the control of the computer. For tomato plants, the carbon dioxide is increased by around four times that of normal fresh air; normal levels are 350ppm and this is increased to 1,200–1,400ppm. The tubes carrying the carbon dioxide are laid alongside the bolsters and extend along the full length of each and every row, increasing the production of the plants.

However, if the vents in the greenhouse open when a problem with humidity occurs, then this increase in carbon dioxide becomes difficult to maintain. The humidity is measured and controlled by the computer. This control is achieved by vapour pressure deficit, that is, raising the temperature of the air as warm air can hold more moisture. The heating pipe temperature is increased, raising the air temperatures. This increase in the temperature of the heating pipes carries on until it gets to the point where the automatic air vents open; changing the air then reducing the humidity. In high humidity, transpiration becomes difficult for the plants and they become more prone to diseases.

In the initial stages, six plants are placed on each bolster, but then each of these plants is allowed the main head plus a second shoot, which gives twelve heads that go up strings from each of the six root systems on one bolster. Strings attached to a secure point beside the bolsters are also attached in a flexible way to an overhead wire high up in the greenhouse. Each plant head is allocated a string, so that as it grows it is taken up to the overhead support wire. When the plant head reaches the top of that string the plant is lowered and fed along and up the string next to it, where it grows up to the overhead wire again. This procedure is carried on as the plant grows. The result is a stem that comes out of the Rockwool cube and by the end of the season can travel 105ft (32m) parallel with the ground before turning and going up the string to the overhead wire.

Each plant head is allowed twenty leaves between the top suspension wire and the lower point. All the lower leaves on the stem travelling along next to the bolsters are removed. This gives the maximum

The plants are grown in double rows spreading out on each side of the road.

The plants on the right are at the beginning of the greenhouse, but the heads will be some distance away.

amount of young, highly productive leaves to draw the water and nutrients up the stem to feed the large trusses of tomatoes.

The grower controls a computer, which regulates the cF, pH, humidity, and feed of carbon dioxide along with the air and solution temperatures. The nutrient is mixed on the spot to one of six formulas. The tap water is tested so that the grower knows which elements, if any, it contains. With this information in mind extra elements are added to match the formulas to be used. The six formulas are used in different stages of growth or conditions. For instance, extra calcium is added early on in the year to prevent end rot in tomatoes. Generally, the formula is adhered to, although deviations do take place on occasions.

Commercial packaging of the produce is just as amazing as the growing. Tomatoes and cucumbers are picked and placed in trays manually. (Both are, of course, grown in separate greenhouses.) They are then taken to large packing sheds where staff feed the tomatoes on to a moving belt. This carries them under a number of electronic cameras, which sense the colour of the tomatoes (the degree of ripeness). Another moving belt takes them further on and they are electronically weighed. They are then dispatched like letters in a sorting office (but not quite so fast) into ports and sorted according to the colour (ripeness) and size (weight). This results in three or four colour grades of a large size and another three or four colour grades of a smaller size.

Tomatoes are sorted by weight and colour and dispatched like letters to boxes.

Cucumbers are wrapped, sealed and packed.

Cucumbers are also picked manually and the straight ones are placed on a moving belt that has troughs across and along its width. A machine draws in cling film from above and below the cucumbers, then chops and seals each one; they move on further and are then subjected to a set temperature for a very short time which shrinks the cling film round the cucumber. These products are then dispatched in cooled transport.

For the amateur wishing to use small numbers of Rockwool slabs it would be best to use intermittent flood and drain instead of drip feed. It is less prone to problems unless the grower is prepared to buy good drip-feed equipment. A small pump from a hydroponic supplier working on a seven on–seven off timer, which can be adjusted, will do the job. Submersible pumps (240V 4W) are usually used for twenty-four-hour working in small systems. The solution is pumped up into the bolster with a timer controlling the pump. The on-period for the timer is set to flood the bolster and slits in the bolster allow the solution to drain back to the main tank which contains the solution and pump. The timer and the size of the drainage slots are adjusted to meet the needs of the system. This would be a recirculating system or 'closed' system.

One problem with Rockwool is the disposal of old slabs. It will not break down in the soil and it cannot be burnt. It can however be reused after sterilization. Small bits can be sterilized in a microwave and used again the next year.

Glossary

Aeroponics
Systems having the roots of the plant in a continuous or intermittent mist of solution and air.

Buffers
Buffers are solutions that resist pH changes. These can be added to the solution to try to keep fluctuation to a minimum. Buffers are used to calibrate pH probes.

Capillary mat
A thicker material than spreader mat, with good capillary action and good water-holding properties. Not used in hydroponics but tends to be confused with spreader mat.

Chelated
A co-ordination compound in which a central metallic ion is attached to an organic molecule at two or more positions. Chelated compounds are available to plants at a much broader range of pH values. They are also more soluble in water.

Chemical compound
Potassium and nitrate form potassium nitrate (two elements chemically attached forming something different). The compound potassium nitrate is used in the nutrient solution, as is calcium nitrate.

Conductivity Factor (cF)
A method of comparing the concentration (strength) of a solution by using a meter to measure the flow of current in the solution. Indicates only the total concentration of the solution and *not* the individual nutrient components. The unit is the cF. Note: Conductivity Factor (cF), Electrical Conductivity (EC) and parts per million (ppm), can all be measured using an appropriately calibrated meter.

One meter with three calibration scales on can give a reading in all three formats. A reading of cF2 is the same as 0.2EC, which is the same as 140ppm.

Electrical Conductivity (EC)
See Conductivity Factor (cF).

Hydroponics
A method of growing plants intensively without soil while feeding the plant roots with all its requirements (soilless culture).

Inert medium
Chemically inactive. Does not contain any nutrients.

Medium
Materials that will hold nutrients, air and water. Normally supplied loose, in blocks or in plastic bolsters. The medium must allow the pH to be controlled.

Nutrient Film Technique (NFT)
The plant's roots are placed directly on to a flat surface, which has a very thin film of nutrient passing over it. Part of the root surface is in the nutrient, but the root system developing above it has only a film of nutrient over it. The roots receive plenty of oxygen, water and nutrients. A growing medium is not used.

Nutrients
Mineral elements required by living plants. Referred to as major nutrients and trace nutrients. Major nutrients are required in relatively large quantities; nitrogen, calcium, phosphate, magnesium, and sulphur are major nutrients. Trace nutrients are required in very much smaller quantities

but are very important. These are iron, manganese, zinc, copper, chlorine, boron (borax) and molybdenum. Other elements are taken from the normal environment.

Parts per million (ppm)
A means of expressing the concentration of individual nutrients in a solution. If 1ml of water weighs 1g, then 1g of potassium nitrate in 1,000,000ml of distilled water would give water with one part per million of potassium nitrate. So 1ppm is 1g in 1,000l (1,000ml in 1l × 1,000 = 1,000,000).

A nutrient salts meter (EC or cF) can be calibrated in ppm as well. cF2 = 0.2 EC = 140ppm. If this were a mix of salts, it would not show the ppm of each.

See also Conductivity Factor (cF).

Photosynthesis
The process that takes place when energy from sunlight comes in contact with the leaves of a plant. Carbon dioxide in the air and water are combined to form sugars (carbohydrates), the plant's basic food. Oxygen is released from the leaves in this process.

Potential Hydrogen (pH)
Small concentrations of hydrogen ions resulting in changes in the acidity or alkalinity of a solution. It is usually referred to on a range of 1 to 14, with 7 being neutral, 1 acid and 14 alkaline.

Precipitance
Two or more useful salts joining to form something the plant cannot use or absorb.

Recirculating systems; Closed systems
Nutrient is continuously pumped around the same system. This can be NFT or a system using a medium. Care must be taken to ensure that the solution does not become unbalanced.

Respiration
During photosynthesis the plants form carbohydrates. The carbohydrates are converted into complex starches to store for use later. The starches are then broken down to release the energy; this is respiration. Carbon dioxide and water are released during this process.

Root mat
The roots intertwine with each other over the tray, and the root mat gradually becomes thicker and thicker. Roots at the bottom will be in the solution, while the roots above will have a film of solution over them by capillary action along with moist air.

Run-to-waste; Non-recirculating; Open
All refer to systems that are usually drip-fed with a 25 per cent solution in excess of the plant's needs; the surplus runs to waste. The excess solution ensures that the nutrient balance around the roots of the plants is maintained throughout the life of the plant.

Spreader mat
A very thin mat made of fibreglass is placed on the base of the channel. This accepts the trickle of solution from the pump, absorbing it and ensuring it is spread across the width of the whole channel. Any material able to wick the solution across the tray that is not phytotoxic will do. It will only be required for a few weeks, then the roots themselves will spread the solution. Do not use a material that will form a gelatinous substance when disintegrating. Hydroponic suppliers sell lengths of spreader mat around 8in (20.3cm) wide. A spreader mat is nothing to do with a capillary mat; capillary matting is usually relatively thick.

Transpiration
The ability of the plant to pass the water taken up by osmosis into the air around the leaves.

Useful Addresses

Defenders Ltd
Occupation Road
Wye
Ashford
Kent
TN25 5EN
Tel: 01233 813121
Fax: 01233 813633
Email: help@defenders.co.uk
Website: www.defenders.co.uk
(Natural predators.)

Futuregrow magazine
PO Box 29
Aberystwyth
SY25 6WG
Tel/fax: 01974 821555
Email: weed1@dircon.co.uk
(Natural predators.)

Green Gardener
41 Strumpshaw Road
Brundall
Norfolk
NR13 5PG
Tel: 01603 715096
Email: advice@greengardener.co.uk
Website: www.greengardener.co.uk
(Natural predators.)

Terry Grimshaw
Independent Hydroponics Consultant and
    Supplier
Hydroman International
31 Park Avenue
Hartsholme
Lincoln
LN6 0BY
Tel: 01522 874363
Email: Tgrimshaw@aol.com

Growell Hydroponics & Plant Lighting Ltd
Jardinerie Garden Centre
Kenilworth Road
Hampton-in-Arden
Solihull
B92 0LW
Tel: 01675 443 950
Fax: 01675 443 951
Freephone: 0800 3281339
Email: info@growell.co.uk
Website: www.growell.co.uk

Growth Technology Limited
Fremantle House
Unit 66
Taunton Trading Estate
Norton Fitzwarren
Taunton
TA2 6RX
Tel: 01823 325291
Fax: 01823 325487
Email: sales@growthtechnology.com
Website: www.growthtechnology.com
(Hydroponic supplies.)

Handmade ceramics/garden sculpture
Keith Bridgewood
Email: keith@bridgewood.karoo.co.uk

HydroGarden Wholesale Supplies Ltd
PO Box 605
Coventry
West Midlands
CV2 5WB
Tel: 024 76612888
Fax: 024 76615888
Email: info@hydrogarden.co.uk
Website: www.hydrogarden.co.uk
(Wholesale supplies only.)

The Kitchen Garden Magazine Ltd
12 Orchard Lane
Woodnewton
Peterborough
PE8 5EE
Tel: 01780 470 097
Fax: 01780 470 550
Website: www.kitchengarden.co.uk

Maplin Electronics
Freepost NEA9433
Barnsley
S73 0BR
Tel: 0870 264 6000
Fax: 0870 264 6001
Website: www.maplin.co.uk
(Temperature modules.)
(The freepost is for UK only. The website has full details.)

John McLauchlan Horticulture
50A Market Place
Thirsk
North Yorkshire
YO7 1LH
Tel: 01845 525585
Fax: 01845 523133
Email: horticulture@jmcl.freeserve.co.uk
Website: www.viresco-uk.com
(Micro-organism products.)

Just Green
Unit 14 Springfield Road Industrial Estate
Burnham-on-Crouch
Essex
CM0 8UA
Tel: 01621 785088
Fax: 01621 783800
Email: sales@just-green.com
Website: www.just-green.com
(Natural predators)

Nutriculture Ltd
Hydroponic Centre
Unit B1A
Towngate Works
Dark Lane
Mawdesley
L40 2QU
Tel: 01704 822536
Fax: 01704 822573
Email: sales@nutriculture.com
Website: www.nutriculture.com

Practical Hydroponics & Greenhouses
PO Box 225
Narrabeen
NSW 2101
Australia
Email: casper@hydroponics.com.au
Website: www.hydroponics.com.au

Index